Jesus and Life
Word Pictures in John's Gospel

John's Gospel comes out of the Jewish world into the Roman world at the end of the first century. Jesus the Jew is the Saviour of the world. He transcends time and place and yet belongs to a particular time and place. In the third decade of the twenty-first century the personal affirmations Jesus makes and the parables Jesus speaks in John's Gospel still ring true.

Published by
Grace & Peace Books
4A Wurilba Ave Hawthorn SA 5062 Australia
djrowston@gmail.com

© 2010 Douglas James Rowston

All rights reserved. This publication is copyright. Photographs were taken by the author. Other than for the purposes of and subject to the conditions of the Copyright Act, no part of it may in any form or by any means (electronic, mechanical, microcopying, photocopying, recording or otherwise) be reproduced, stored in a retrieval system or transmitted without prior written permission from the publisher.

First published 2010 by BCSA. This edition published in 2021.

ISBN 978-0-6453288-1-3
1. Jesus Christ—Biblical teaching.
2. Bible. N.T. John—Criticism, interpretation, etc.
226.5

Acknowledgements

Bible quotations are from the New Revised Standard Version Bible, Anglicized Edition, copyright © 1989, 1995 by the Division of Christian Education of the National Council of Churches of Christ in the U S A. Used by permission. All rights reserved.

The ink sketches were drawn by his colleague Craig Bowyer during the author's time of teaching at Prince Alfred College in Adelaide.

This book is dedicated to Rosalie

Contents

Introduction 1

The 'I am' Sayings of Jesus

1. The Bread of Life 7
2. The Light of the World 11
3. Before Abraham 15
4. The Gate for the Sheep 19
5. The Good Shepherd 23
6. The Resurrection and the Life 29
7. The Way, the Truth, the Life 35
8. The True Vine 39

The Parables of Eternal Life

9. The Night Breeze 43
10. The Bridegroom and the Best Man 47
11. The Ripe Fields 51
12. The Apprentice Son 55
13. The Slave and the Son 59
14. The Shepherd and the Stranger 63
15. The Traveller in the Dark 67
16. The Grain of Wheat 71
17. The Walker at Sunset 75
18. The Bathtub and the Basin 79
19. The Father's House 83
20. The Woman in Childbirth 87

Postscript 91
Select Bibliography 93

Introduction

Jesus and Life

The importance of Jesus in human history and the reality of God's kind of life in human experience are summed up in the most famous verse in the Bible: *For God so loved the world that he gave his only Son, so that everyone who believes in him may not perish but may have eternal life.(John 3:16)*

In John's Gospel Jesus is all about life.

The major theme of the Gospels of Matthew, Mark, and Luke is the kingdom of God. On the other hand, the major theme of John's Gospel is eternal life, God's kind of life. God's rule and eternal life are already present in Jesus' first coming and will be fully realised in Jesus' second coming. Between the first and second comings we are to trust and obey the Lord. As the Fourth Gospel says, the signs of Jesus' ministry *are written so that you may come to believe that Jesus is the Messiah, the Son of God, and that through believing you may have life in his name.(John 20:31)*

By calling this book *Jesus and Life* I am making the point that John's Gospel is applicable to the lives of its first hearers and readers, and is certainly applicable to our lives. Back then and right now the Gospel tells its readers that Jesus *came that they may have life, and have it abundantly.(John 10:10)*

The dynamic nature of the Fourth Gospel is evident in the combination of sayings and deeds of Jesus, the memories of his disciples, and the guidance of his Spirit. The publication of the Gospel fulfils the promise of Jesus: *I have said these things to you while I am still with you. But the Advocate, the Holy Spirit, whom the Father will send in my name, will teach you everything, and remind you of all that I have said to you.(John 14:25-26)* As we read John's Gospel we are in touch with Jesus himself, the first followers of Jesus, and the Spirit of truth.

According to the Fourth Gospel, everything people look for in bread and light, shepherd and vine is ultimately to be found only in Jesus. Jesus doesn't identify a type of ethical teaching or a kind of doctrinal viewpoint or a system of religion with the real thing. He is saying that he himself is the real thing, Life with a capital L! Unfortunately, John hints, too many people are satisfied with pale imitations of the real thing!

Word Pictures

The subtitle of this book is based on the fact that John's Gospel has an intriguing and meaningful range of word pictures.

The first group of the Fourth Gospel's word pictures parallels sayings about the central theme of the first three Gospels, the kingdom of God which brings God's new order. According to the Gospels of Matthew, Mark, and Luke, Jesus says, 'The kingdom of God is like this and that.' According to John's Gospel, he says, 'I am this and that.' In other words, he is the king of God's kingdom who brings God's kind of life.

In all four Gospels believers see God's kingly activity in Jesus who rescues people from sin and evil. He is the one who begins a new godly community with a new style of living. His people are the ones who share his sufferings, know his resurrection power, and look forward to his final victory. God's rule and God's kind of life have begun to be realised in the life of Jesus of Nazareth and will be fully realised in the final victory of Jesus the Lord.

The Fourth Gospel includes eight **'I am' sayings of Jesus** with three particular features. They describe the identity of Jesus. They list requirements of followers of Jesus. They give promises to followers of Jesus.

The eight 'I am' sayings in John's Gospel are as follows:

6:35	The Bread of Life
8:12	The Light of the World
8:58	Before Abraham
10:7, 9	The Gate for the Sheep
10:11, 14-15	The Good Shepherd
11:25-26	The Resurrection and the Life
14:6-7	The Way, the Truth, the Life
15:1-2, 5	The True Vine

The second group of the Fourth Gospel's word pictures is akin to the parables of the first three Gospels. The parables compare everyday events with events of eternal importance. They are stories from real life. They challenge the listeners to stop and think about what they are doing with their lives. In such a parable everything is focussed on a single meaning. The parables of Jesus comment upon the meaning of God's kingdom in the life of Jesus. They remain literary masterpieces with perennial relevance.

In simple terms, the parables of the first three Gospels fall into four groups. Some are about the coming and growth of God's kingdom. God's rule comes and grows in the work of Jesus. Others are about the grace and mercy of God's kingdom. The grace and mercy of God's rule extend to all. Some are about the citizens of God's kingdom. The citizens of God's rule are God's kind of people. Others are about the crisis of God's kingdom. Decisions for and against God's rule are crucial here and hereafter.

The Fourth Gospel includes a dozen **parables of eternal life** which compare life in the spiritual order with life in the physical order.

The parables of eternal life in John's Gospel are as follows:

3:8	The Night Breeze
3:29	The Bridegroom and the Best Man
4:35-38	The Ripe Fields
5:19-20a	The Apprentice Son
8:35	The Slave and the Son
10:1-5	The Shepherd and the Stranger
11:9-10	The Traveller in the Dark
12:24	The Grain of Wheat
12:35-36	The Walker at Sunset
13:10	The Bathtub and the Basin
14:2-3	The Father's House
16:21	The Woman in Childbirth

When we look at both the 'I am' sayings and the parables of eternal life in John's Gospel some observations of Eduard Schweizer are relevant.

First, Jesus uses everyday language and connects with his hearers when and where they live.

Second, such everyday language of Jesus can only be understood by hearers who get involved personally.

Third, the word pictures in all four Gospels are exaggerated at times and are focussed on Jesus, God's kingdom, or God's kind of life.

Fourth, the teaching of Jesus involves continuing education for the believer in the community of faith.

Fifth, acceptance of the message of Jesus opens up the future. According to Matthew, Mark, and Luke, the kingdom of God starts to live in the followers of Jesus. According to John, the believer abides in someone who is the same yesterday, today, and for ever.

Finally, what is latent or implicit in the first three Gospels is patent or explicit in the fourth Gospel. The Gospels of Matthew, Mark, and Luke make comparisons of God's kingdom, John's Gospel gives definitions of Jesus, the king of God's kingdom who brings God's kind of life.

How to utilise this book

This book is designed to be read by individuals or groups as an introduction to key sayings in John's Gospel.

An individual may use it as a collection of devotional studies over an extended period of time. Once a week or so we may 'hear, read, mark, learn, and inwardly digest' a revered part of the Holy Scriptures known as John's Gospel.

A home group may work through a series of Bible Studies on a weekly or fortnightly basis. Members of the group may take it in turns to lead the times of discussion and prayer.

Each short chapter includes the following:
>the key text;
>its context;
>its content, in detailed and summarised format ;
>connections, with questions for reflection and discussion;
>time for prayer, with an example of a short prayer.

My prayer for readers of this book is as follows:
>*Shed upon your Church, O Lord,*
>*the brightness of your light,*
>*so that we, being illumined by the teaching*
>*of John the evangelist,*
>*may walk in the light of your truth,*
>*and be brought to the fullness of eternal life*
>*through Jesus Christ our Lord,*
>*who lives and reigns with you and the Holy Spirit,*
>*one God, for ever and ever. Amen.*

1 The Bread of Life

What do we enjoy when we enter a bakery? We may enjoy the allure of iced coffee or chutney in corned beef sandwiches or freshly cooked coffee scrolls. But we would have to admit that we need bread more than we need iced coffee or fruit chutney or coffee scrolls. Nothing surpasses the goodness of wholesome hot bread. It's the same with life. Everyone needs to distinguish between basic needs and desirable wants.

Key Text

I am the bread of life.
Whoever comes to me will never be hungry,
and whoever believes in me will never be thirsty.
(John 6:35).

Context of Key Text in John 6:25-40: 'The Bread from Heaven'

John 6 describes a sign of Jesus when he feeds about five thousand people with bread and fish and then explains the sign with reference to the bread's source, nature, and reception. The source of the bread of God *is my Father who gives you the true bread from heaven.(John 6:32)* The nature of the bread is found in Jesus, *the living bread that came down from heaven.(John 6:51)* The reception of the bread is mixed. Some do believe, others choose not to do so. Many said, *This teaching is difficult; who can accept it?(John 6:60)* The sign occurs at the time of Passover (John 6:4) and the explanation is given in the synagogue at Capernaum (John 6:59).

Content of Key Text

Detail   Jesus' hearers had seen him feed five thousand at Passover time. The original Passover took place during the time of Moses (Exodus 12-13) and led to the escape from Egypt, the journey through the wilderness, the giving of the law at Sinai, and the entry into Canaan.

The people whom Jesus miraculously fed would have known of two events in the time of Moses. First was the gift of manna. *In the evening quails came up and covered the camp; and in the morning there was a layer of dew around the camp. When the layer of dew lifted, there on the surface of the wilderness was a fine flaky substance, as fine as frost on the ground. When the Israelites saw it, they said to one another, 'What is it?' For they did not know what it was. Moses said to them, 'It is the bread that the LORD has given you to eat.'(Exodus 16:13-15)* Second was the provision of water from the rock. *Moses took the staff from before the LORD, as he had commanded him. Moses and Aaron gathered the assembly together before the rock, and he said to them, 'Listen, you rebels, shall we bring water for you out of this rock?' Then Moses lifted up his hand and struck the rock twice with his staff; water came out abundantly, and the congregation and their livestock drank. (Numbers 20:9-11)*

By the time of Jesus people appear to have believed that the coming Messiah, the second Redeemer, would correspond to Moses, the first Redeemer, because the miracle of the manna had to be repeated in the age to come. The people whom Jesus miraculously fed would have asked some questions. Is Jesus a new Moses? Is Jesus the Messiah of God? Is Jesus doing what only God can do? Is Jesus the life giving bread himself?

Jesus answers such questions. *I am the bread of life. Whoever comes to me will never be hungry, and whoever believes in me will never be thirsty.* Jesus sounds like the Old Testament figure of Wisdom who issues an invitation: *Come, eat of my bread and drink of the wine I have mixed. Lay aside immaturity, and live, and walk in the way of insight.(Proverbs 9:5-6)* Jesus offers the food and drink of instruction and insight. Jesus also sounds like a teacher of wisdom from the second century BC. Ben Sira had said that people can never get too much wisdom. *Come to me, you who desire me, and eat your fill of my fruits. For the memory of me is sweeter than honey, and the possession of me sweeter than the honeycomb. Those who eat of me will hunger for more, and those who drink of me will thirst for more.(Sirach 24:19-21)* Jesus is hinting that people who come to him and believe in him will only hunger and thirst for his teaching. This is a healthy hunger and thirst! It's the basic requirement of Jesus that we should hunger and thirst for his teaching.

The teachers of wisdom had said that God feeds people with his revealed truth. According to John Jesus is God's Word and the Bread of Life. Jesus himself is the bread of life. Jesus himself satisfies the deepest human needs. The bread of which he talks is not a commodity which he supplies, it is Jesus himself. He is promising his nourishing presence in the life of believers. Jesus has come to give life in its fullness. What we need for real life is available in Jesus. The bread of the ordinary person kept coming daily, but Jesus the bread of life came once.

Summary The people whom Jesus miraculously fed would have known of the gift of manna and the provision of water in the wilderness. They would have asked some questions. Is Jesus a new Moses? Is Jesus the Messiah of God? Is Jesus doing what only God can do? Is he the life giving bread himself? In reply, Jesus identifies himself, requires something of his hearers, and promises something to them.

Connections

(a) Everyone has basic needs. We need food, shelter, clothing, and work, but we may want a feast, a mansion, a wardrobe.
* How do we distinguish basic needs and desirable wants?
(b) In ancient times people worshipped false gods. But in modern times we have come of age and don't worship such false gods ... or do we!?
* Who or what are pale imitations of Jesus the real thing in our lives?
(c) When Jesus talks about bread he is referring to the essential diet of most people in Roman Palestine. Bread provided half of the kilojoules or calories available to peasants in the time of Jesus.
* How does bread point to what Jesus essentially requires of us and what Jesus encouragingly promises to us?

Time for Prayer

Lord, our living bread, we thank you for food in a world where many are hungry, for faith in a world where many are fearful, and for friends in a world where many are lonely. Amen.

2 The Light of the World

When my children were young, they used to enjoy seeing the lights of Adelaide as we drove home through the hills. The lights became known as 'fairyland'. They lit up the dark of the surrounding suburbs and made a lovely view, especially at the end of a long journey home from visiting relatives in Melbourne. When Jesus told his disciples that he was the light of the world he was giving a meaningful word picture about finding the way in the midst of a dark and threatening world.

Key Text

I am the light of the world.
Whoever follows me will never walk in darkness
but will have the light of life.
(John 8:12)

Context of Key Text in John 8:12-20: 'Jesus the Light of the World'

John 8 is about Jesus as the judge of life. It begins with the claim of Jesus to be the light. Jesus is in the Temple at the Feast of Tabernacles. During the festival the lighting of four giant lampstands in the Temple recalled the pillar of fire which led the Israelites out of Egypt and the daily procession of people bringing water from Siloam symbolised the future outpouring of the Messianic Spirit. Against this background Jesus is speaking to Jewish leaders who resist his claims regarding his origin and his destiny.

Content of Key Text

Detail Then and now at the Feast of Tabernacles or Booths Jewish people build huts outside their homes to remember the wilderness wandering under the leadership of Moses. As Leviticus 23:42-43 commands: *You shall live in booths for seven days; all that are citizens in Israel shall live in booths, so that your generations may know that I made the people of Israel live in booths when I brought them out of the land of Egypt: I am the LORD your God.*

At Tabernacles in John 7 and 8 Jesus is claiming a unique status. Jesus is the prophet greater than Moses mentioned in Deuteronomy 18:15, *The LORD your God will raise up for you a prophet like me from among your own people.* Jesus is the Messiah who gives the Spirit. In the previous chapter he had said, *Let anyone who is thirsty come to me, and let the one who believes in me drink. As the scripture has said, 'Out of the believer's heart shall flow rivers of living water.'(John 7:37-38)* Jesus is the pillar of fire leading God's people out of the land of sin and death into the land of righteousness and life: *I am the light of the world. Whoever follows me will never walk in darkness but will have the light of life.* Jesus is the light and gives the light.

Jesus is also laying down a wonderful promise: *Whoever follows me will never walk in darkness but will have the light of life.* Jesus brings light and life. Light is God in action according to Psalm 44:3, *Not by their own sword did they win the land, nor did their own arm give them victory; but your right hand, and your arm, and the light of your countenance.* How do we see God in action?

If Jesus is our light and life, we fulfil the promises of Isaiah of Babylon. *I am the LORD, I have called you in righteousness, I have taken you by the hand and kept you; I have given you as a covenant to the people, a light to the nations, to open the eyes that are blind ... I will give you as a light to the nations, that my salvation may reach to the end of the earth.(Isaiah 42:6-7; 49:6)* If Jesus is our light and life, we become light to the world. And this is all because of Jesus. *In him was life, and the life was the light of all people. The light shines in the darkness, and the darkness did not overcome it.(John 1:4-5)* Yes, the Eternal Word is offering himself as life and light, changing and saving true believers.

Finally, Jesus is setting out an important requirement: *Whoever follows me will never walk in darkness but will have the light of life.* Jesus is the light to be followed. If we live in darkness, we miss the growth, the health, the goodness which light brings. If the man born blind in John 9 had not followed the light, he would have missed the power and truth of God. In fact, he did follow the light and was able to say, *One thing I do know, that though I was blind, now I see.(John 9:25)*

A famous scholar was right when he said, 'The disciples are the light of the world only inasmuch as they reflect Jesus.' In Matthew 5 the same idea occurs, *You are the light of the world ... Let your light shine before others, so that they may ... give glory to your Father in heaven.(Matthew 5:14, 16)*

Summary Against the background of the Feast of Tabernacles Jesus claims to be the prophet greater than Moses, the Messiah who gives the Spirit, the pillar of fire leading God's people from death to life. He promises his followers light and life and requires them to reflect the light and share the life of their Lord.

Connections

(a) Sometimes people experience through severe loss or deep depression or real temptation a 'dark night of the soul'. At such times the contrast between emptiness of the dark and fullness of the light recalls the forsaken feelings of Jesus on the cross.
* Have we heard of someone who has experienced the 'dark night of the soul'?
(b) The presence of light results in life even in the face of death. In suffering and hope believers follow the one who died on Good Friday and was raised on Easter Sunday. Light is God in action. He smiles upon his creation morning by morning. He smiles upon his people day by day.
* What does light symbolise?
(c) The message of Jesus includes gift and demand. He gives salvation as God's gift, the saving power to receive God's kind of life. He also gives salvation as God's demand, the saving power to live God's kind of life.
* What does light show us that Jesus promises to us and requires of us?

Time for Prayer

Lord, our life giving light, without you we are living in the dark of evil and death and without you we lack purpose and meaning. Jesus, we need you. Give us your light and life. Amen.

3 Before Abraham

In today's world, there are true and false ideas about Jesus. Did he ever live? He most certainly did. But, was he an ethical teacher, or an apocalyptic prophet, or a wandering cynic, or a revolutionary leader, or a meek and mild holy man, or something else? Fortunately, with the help of the faith community and the educational academy we can read John 8 to find some true ideas about Jesus.

Key Text

Very truly, I tell you, before Abraham was, I am.
(John 8:58)

Context of Key Text in John 8:48-59: 'Jesus and Abraham'

As we have seen, John 8 is about Jesus as the judge of life. The chapter features the claim of Jesus to be judge. Jesus is in the Temple and is speaking to the Jewish leaders, who are not likely to respond in faith. The issue is the question who Jesus is. The opponents of Jesus ask him, *Who do you claim to be? (John 8:53)* In reply, Jesus draws a contrast between Abraham and himself. The opponents attempt to stone Jesus because of his controversial reply that he is prior to Abraham, father of the faithful and friend of God.

Content of Key Text

Detail   Jesus begins by saying *Very truly*, literally, *Amen, amen,* or 'Let it be, let it be'. Normally the word Amen is used at the end of a solemn statement as in prayer. Jesus uses it at the beginning of a solemn statement and he doubles its use. It is almost as though he is saying, 'Thus says the Lord' in the tradition of the Old Testament prophets.

According to John, Jesus makes a really significant contrast between the highly honoured ancestor Abraham and the very controversial prophet who has come from Nazareth to Jerusalem. The difference between the tenses of the verbs in this verse *before Abraham **was**, I **am*** means that before Abraham came into being, Jesus existed eternally. It is a dramatic claim to the divinity of Jesus. The Gospel had begun with the same ideas about Jesus the Word: *In the beginning was the Word, and the Word was with God, and the Word was God. He was in the beginning with God. All things came into being through him.(John 1:1-3)*

The words *I am* may recall an incident in the Old Testament. *God said to Moses, 'I AM WHO I AM.' He said further, 'Thus you shall say to the Israelites, "I AM has sent me to you."'(Exodus 3:14) 'I AM WHO I AM'* is a verbal phrase based on the verb 'to be'. It points towards God's eternal being. He is always there.

The Exodus passage may have influenced Isaiah of Babylon, who speaks of God in a similar way. *I, the LORD, am first, and will be with the last.(Isaiah 41:4b) You are my witnesses, says the LORD, and my servant whom I have chosen, so that you may know and believe me and understand that I am he ... I am God, and also henceforth I am He.(Isaiah 43:10a, 13a)*

I AM is the self designation of God in Exodus. *I am He* is spoken only by God in Isaiah. *I am* is spoken only by Jesus in John. All of this leads the believer to understand that Jesus the Son of God is one with the Father, yet God remains one. The opponents' lack of insight hinders their acceptance of Jesus as the human face of God. They do not realise that Jesus not only reveals God but also obeys God.

The close relationship between Jesus and God is also evident in Matthew 11, a passage which has been described as 'a meteorite out of the Johannine heaven'. *All things have been handed over to me by my Father; and no one knows the Son except the Father, and no one knows the Father except the Son and anyone to whom the Son chooses to reveal him.(Matthew 11:27)* John's Gospel in its use of *I am* makes explicit what is implicit in Matthew's Gospel.

Summary Jesus is making a solemn statement about who he is. Whereas Abraham came into being, Jesus existed eternally. His use of *I am* recalls God in Exodus and Isaiah. He is claiming to be the human face of God. The close relationship between Jesus and God in John 8:58 is paralleled in Matthew 11:27.

Connections

(a) Abraham is important for Jews, Christians, and Muslims.
Jews see him as their ancestor through Isaac.
Christians remember that he believed God and God reckoned it to him as righteousness.
Muslims honour him as their ancestor through Ishmael.
* Who was Abraham and what was his significance?

(b) The names of God are many and varied.

In the Hebrew Old Testament divine names include Elohim (God) and Yahweh (The LORD). In Exodus *I AM* is related to Yahweh.

In the Greek New Testament divine names include Theos (God) and Kurios (Lord). On occasions both names are applied to Jesus.

Finally, Allah, the Muslim name for God, is simply Arabic for 'the God'.

* What is the background of the words *I am*?

(c) Through the years Christianity has struggled to balance the divinity and the humanity of Jesus.

In the church councils of the fourth and fifth centuries Jesus was identified as truly divine, truly human, indivisibly divine and human, having two natures united in one person.

Mainline churches of today seek to apply these insights in order to avoid unbalanced views of Jesus which are propagated by heretical groups.

* What was Jesus claiming and how does it affect us today?

Time for Prayer

Lord, we think of Abraham, the friend of God and the father of the faithful. And then we give thanks for Jesus the eternal one and the fulfilment of all Abraham's hopes. Amen.

4 The Gate for the Sheep

When I was a younger Christian, there were some popular sacred songs about sheep and gates. One was sung by a middle aged baritone named George Beverley Shea, 'There were ninety and nine that safely lay in the shelter of the fold, but one was out on the hills away, far off from the gates of gold.' Another was sung by a pretty blonde named Evie, 'He the pearly gates will open, so that I may enter in; for he purchased my redemption and forgave me all my sin.'

Key Text

Very truly, I tell you, I am the gate for the sheep ...
I am the gate.
Whoever enters by me will be saved,
and will come in and go out and find pasture.
(John 10:7, 9)

Context of Key Text in John 10:7-10: 'Jesus the Gate'

The first half of John 10 is about Jesus as the shepherd of life. After telling the parable of the shepherd and the stranger (John 10:1-6), Jesus makes his first explanation with the symbolism of the gate, or the door, (John 10:7-10). This symbol reinforces the message of the gathering, guarding, and guiding shepherd of life.

Content of Key Text

Detail Jesus was speaking at the time of the Festival of Dedication (John 10:22). At Dedication, around Christmas time today, Jews celebrate the reconsecration of the Temple in 165 BC after the Syrian King Antiochus IV had profaned it by erecting an altar to Zeus and sacrificing a pig on the altar three years before. This event is mentioned in the Old Testament (Daniel 9:26-27) and the New Testament (Matthew 24:15-16). The whole story is told in the Apocrypha, 1 Maccabees 1-4. The main point is that Dedication was another Tabernacles, a celebration of liberation from a Syrian tyrant, the prototype of a false leader, a thief who comes to steal and kill and destroy.

At such a time Jesus calls himself the door or the gate to the sheep. *Very truly, I tell you, I am the gate for the sheep.* Yet again Jesus begins with *Very truly*, literally, *Amen, amen.* Jesus speaks of regulating access of pastors to the sheep. *All who came before me are thieves and bandits; but the sheep did not listen to them. (John 10:8)* Only true shepherds, his ministers or pastors, have access to the sheep. He also speaks of regulating access of members to the flock: *Whoever enters by me will be saved, and will come in and go out and find pasture.* Only Jesus is the door or the gate for the sheep, the members of his flock, into the sheepfold where the sheep move about freely.

Jesus contrasts himself with false leaders who are known for their stealing and killing and destroying: *The thief comes only to steal and kill and destroy. I came that they may have life, and have it abundantly. (John 10:10)* His listeners could not help but think of the Syrian king who was the desolator of the Temple in Maccabean times or the corrupt high priests of Hasmonean times or the false leaders, political and religious, in Herodian times. Unlike them all, Jesus can be trusted. He is the true liberator. Jesus does not steal. He respects. Jesus does not kill. He gives life. Jesus does not destroy. Rather, *everyone who* believes in him may not perish but may have eternal life. (John 3:16)* In Jesus life overflows with all that is good.

The description of Jesus as the door or the gate leads to the requirement for all who wish to follow Jesus. First, the sheep listen to the true shepherd. This is implicit in the statement: *All who came before me are thieves and bandits; but the sheep did not listen to them. (John 10:8)* Second, the sheep enter through the true door or gate to find salvation. That is explicit in the words: *I am the gate. Whoever enters by me will be saved, and will come in and go out and find pasture.*

The first disciples of Jesus, all of whom were Jewish followers of a Jewish Messiah, would have remembered the words of the Jewish song writer: *Open to me the gates of righteousness, that I may enter through them and give thanks to the LORD. This is the gate of the LORD; the righteous shall enter through it. (Psalm 118:19-20)*

The picture of green pastures portrays the promise of salvation in a moving way for an agrarian society. Pasture is obtained through Jesus the gate. The image is particularly strong if one thinks of a Palestinian shepherd sleeping across the entrance to the sheepfold, giving the sheep safety from the thief, giving the sheep freedom in the fold, and giving sustenance from the provision of feed. This interpretation is supported by the words of Jesus about life: *I came that they may have life, and have it abundantly. (John 10:10)*

Summary Against the background of the Festival of Dedication, a celebration of liberation from a false leader, Jesus contrasts himself with thieves and bandits and calls himself the door or the gate for the sheep into the sheepfold. He requires all who wish to follow him to listen to the true shepherd and to enter through the true door or gate to find salvation. Salvation is obtained through Jesus the door or the gate.

Connections

(a) A door serves as a means of access or exit for a building. A gate opens into a fenced yard or walled town.
* How does the picture of a door or a gate apply to Jesus?
(b) Elsewhere Jesus says, *Enter through the narrow gate; for the gate is wide and the road is easy that leads to destruction, and there are many who take it. For the gate is narrow and the road is hard that leads to life, and there are few who find it. (Matthew 7:13-14)*
* What do the pictures of a narrow gate and a wide gate tell us about Jesus' message?
(c) Jesus speaks of regulating access of pastors to the sheep and of regulating access of members to the fold. A gate or a door can include and exclude. Jesus wants people who model a worthy life. He wants leaders who feed rather than fleece the flock!
* How do we maintain the integrity of pastors and members?

Time for Prayer

Our God, we thank you that Jesus calls himself the gate, when he brings us to you, and that this is not about what happens just when life ends but when life really starts now. Amen.

5 The Good Shepherd

Hagia Sophia in Istanbul was once the largest church in Christendom. Of all the preachers from its pulpit one stands out as the greatest of his time. John, Bishop of Constantinople from 398 to 404, was later called Chrysostom, Greek for 'Golden Mouth'. He described the connection between the two 'I am' sayings *I am the gate* and *I am the good shepherd* in a helpful way. 'When Jesus brings us to the Father he calls himself a door, when he takes care of us, a shepherd.'

Key Text
I am the good shepherd.
The good shepherd lays down his life for the sheep ...
I am the good shepherd.
I know my own and my own know me,
just as the Father knows me and I know the Father.
And I lay down my life for the sheep.
(John 10:11, 14-15)

Context of Key Text in John 10:11-18: 'Jesus the Good Shepherd'

The first half of John 10 is about the shepherd of life. After telling the parable of the shepherd and the stranger (John 10:1-6), Jesus makes his second explanation with the symbolism of the good shepherd (John 10:11-18). This symbol also reinforces the message of the gathering, guarding, and guiding shepherd of life.

I am the good shepherd.

John 10:11

Content of Key Text

Detail   The idea of a good shepherd occurs in the other Gospels too. For example, Jesus says, *What do you think? If a shepherd has a hundred sheep, and one of them has gone astray, does he not leave the ninety-nine on the mountains and go in search of the one that went astray? And if he finds it, truly I tell you, he rejoices over it more than over the ninety-nine that never went astray. (Matthew 18:12-13)*

In the Fourth Gospel *the good* (or model or noble or beautiful or ideal) *shepherd,* has negative and positive connotations.

Negatively, Jesus is called the good shepherd by way of contrast with the political and religious leaders of the people. Beyond the Jewish world, there is also a contrast with shepherd like gods of the pagan world, such as Dionysus, the god of wine, and Hermes, the herald of the gods.

Positively, Jesus is called the good shepherd for two reasons. First, he is willing to die to protect his sheep. Unlike *the hired hand* who *sees the wolf coming and leaves the sheep and runs away (John 10:12)*, the good shepherd says, *I lay down my life for the sheep.* Second, he knows his sheep intimately. *I know my own and my own know me, just as the Father knows me and I know the Father.* The mutual knowledge between shepherd and sheep is compared with the mutual knowledge between Father and Son. By knowledge Jesus is not speaking about knowledge as sight in the sense of contemplation, but knowledge as experience in the sense of covenant.

Elsewhere Jesus had said, *All things have been handed over to me by my Father; and no one knows the Son except the Father, and no one knows the Father except the Son and anyone to whom the Son chooses to reveal him.(Matthew 11:27)*

Jesus looks beyond the Jewish world to the Roman world. *I have other sheep that do not belong to this fold. I must bring them also, and they will listen to my voice. So there will be one flock, one shepherd.(John 10:16)* Jewish and Gentile believers listen to the voice of Jesus to find salvation.

The promise of the good shepherd is to lay down his life for the sheep. In the Fourth Gospel, Jesus promises to do this in three other passages: *And just as Moses lifted up the serpent in the wilderness, so must the Son of Man be lifted up (John 3:14); When you have lifted up the Son of Man, then you will realise that I am he (John 8:28); And I, when I am lifted up from the earth, will draw all people to myself (John 12:32).* Jesus is picking up the theme of Isaiah of Babylon: *See, my servant shall prosper; he shall be exalted and lifted up.(Isaiah 52:13)*

Summary Jesus is called the good shepherd by way of contrast with the political and religious leaders of the Jewish world and with shepherd like gods of the pagan world. Jesus, the good shepherd, is willing to die to protect his sheep and knows his sheep intimately. Jesus is speaking about knowledge not as sight but experience. Jewish and Gentile followers listen to the voice of the true shepherd who lays down his life for the sheep.

Connections

(a) We may contrast the Australian sheep farmer and his sheep dogs, his large flocks on extensive land, his produce of wool or meat with the Palestinian shepherd and his small flock in a sheepfold near his cottage, his produce of milk and wool.
* How do the circumstances of the Palestinian shepherd illuminate the description of Jesus?

(b) Christians who read Psalm 23, 'the Shepherd Psalm', against the background of Jesus, 'the model shepherd' in John 10, have their impressions of Jesus enriched and enlarged.

Psalm 23:1-3 is a meditation in the third person.
> *The Lord is my shepherd ...*
> *He makes me lie down in green pastures;*
> *he leads me beside still waters;*
> *he restores my soul.*
> *He leads me in right paths ...*

Psalm 23:4-6 is a conversation with God in the second person.
> *You are with me;*
> *your rod and your staff ... comfort me.*
> *You prepare a table before me ...*
> *you anoint my head with oil ...*

The last verse of the psalm sets this conversation in a communal context.
> *I shall dwell in the house of the Lord my whole life long.*

* What characteristics does the shepherd of Psalm 23 share with the shepherd of John 10?

(c) The good shepherd looks beyond death. *For this reason the Father loves me, because I lay down my life in order to take it up again. No one takes it from me, but I lay it down of my own accord. I have power to lay it down, and I have power to take it up again.(John 10:17-18)*
* How does the follower of the good shepherd face death? Why is this so?

Time for Prayer

Our God, we thank you that Jesus calls himself the shepherd, when he takes care of us, and that this means that the followers of Jesus have eternal life now as well as for ever. Amen.

6 The Resurrection and the Life

Some years ago a sorrowing widower received a letter including the following helpful words from a former pastor: 'I have no words of explanation - only great sadness and empathy for you and your loved ones. I have found in my "valleys of the shadows" that I was mysteriously and graciously sustained and I am confident that will occur for you as well .... But I have more reason than ever to believe in the Resurrection. When we get to the place where we have to say: "If there is any thing more, it is up to God," I have found there is more.'

Key Text

I am the resurrection and the life.
Those who believe in me, even though they die, will live,
and everyone who lives and believes in me will never die.
(John 11:25-26)

Context of Key Text in John 11:17-27: 'Jesus the Resurrection and the Life'

John 11 is about Jesus the resurrection and the life. It relates the story of the death of Lazarus at Bethany. After Jesus has told the disciples the parable of the traveller in the dark, they reach the home of Lazarus. Jesus meets Martha, one of the sisters of Lazarus, and calls forth her belief in Jesus as the Messiah and the Son of God. Mary, the other sister of Lazarus, joins Martha and Jesus. They all go to the tomb of Lazarus and Jesus calls forth the dead man.

*I am the resurrection and the life.
Those who believe in me, even though they die, will live,
and everyone who lives and believes in me will never die.*

John 11:25-26

Content of Key Text

Detail Elsewhere Jesus promises that God's kind of life is enjoyed here and now by believers. *Very truly, I tell you, anyone who hears my word and believes him who sent me has eternal life, and does not come under judgment, but has passed from death to life. Very truly, I tell you, the hour is coming, and is now here, when the dead will hear the voice of the Son of God, and those who hear will live.(John 5:24-25)*

The same power which gives believers eternal life during their earthly existence will, after the death of the body, give renewed existence in the life beyond. *Do not be astonished at this; for the hour is coming when all who are in their graves will hear his voice and will come out—those who have done good, to the resurrection of life, and those who have done evil, to the resurrection of condemnation.(John 5:28-29)* The account of John 11 makes the same points as John 5.

Before Lazarus returns (temporarily) from the dead, Jesus talks with Martha. Jesus assures Martha, *Your brother will rise again.(John 11:23)* Martha affirms the popular Jewish expectation, *I know that he will rise again in the resurrection on the last day.(John 11:24)* Then Jesus brings future expectation into present experience. *I am the resurrection and the life.*

Resurrection for the Jew meant an embodied and new life for the dead after they have been asleep awaiting the judgment. For the Christian it came to mean the embodied and new life for the crucified Jesus. And it will mean the resurrection of all at the final coming of Christ. *Life* for the Jew meant the gift of the creating and sustaining God to all persons and things. For the Christian it came to mean the new life inaugurated and realised by the coming of Jesus and the gift of the Holy Spirit. In simple terms, it's eternal life, God's kind of life.

First, Jesus focuses on the effect of faith on the believer's death. As the resurrection, Jesus is saying that he gives spiritual life to the physically dead. Second, Jesus focuses on the effect of faith on the believer's life. As the life, Jesus is saying that he does not allow spiritual death to touch those who believe in him. William Barclay's translation captures the meaning well: 'In death to believe in me is to live again. In life, for any man (or woman), to believe in me is never to die.'

Subsequently Martha responds to Jesus, *Lord, I believe that you are the Messiah, the Son of God, the one coming into the world.(John 11:27)* To call Jesus Messiah, Son of God, and the Coming One, is to identify him as the priestly king, the one who obeys and reveals God, and the fulfilment of God's promises.

It should be noted that the temporary resuscitation of Lazarus can be understood to prefigure the final resurrection of the dead. The actual resurrection of Jesus, on the other hand, is the first instalment of the final resurrection of the dead. In the words of Paul, *Christ, being raised from the dead, will never die again (Romans 6:9)* and *Christ has been raised from the dead, the first fruits of those who have died (1 Corinthians 15:20).*

Summary In John 5 Jesus promises that God's kind of life is enjoyed here and now by believers and that God's power will, after the death of the body, give renewed existence in the life beyond. John 11 makes the same points. Jesus, *the resurrection and the life*, brings future expectation into present experience. Jesus focuses on the effect of faith on the believer's death. Jesus also focuses on the effect of faith on the believer's life.

Connections

(a) When we experience a severe loss, we go through grief and experience uncomfortable emotions such as shock, anger, guilt, and depression before we manage to cope and go on with life.
* How and why does our key text give us the basis of hope in the face of a severe loss?
(b) The disciples did not understand Jesus when he spoke gently of Lazarus' death as a falling asleep. They may have been in a state of denial. Martha and Mary idolised their dead brother, Lazarus. They may have felt the need to elevate Lazarus to immediate sainthood.
* What can we do instead of being stuck in denial or being unreal?
(c) In his treatment of the characters in John 11, Alan Culpepper tentatively has suggested that Martha represents the ideal of faith and service, Mary love and devotion, Lazarus resurrection hope.
* What is the evidence for these characterisations?

Time for Prayer

Lord Jesus, you are the resurrection and the life. We, as your followers, thank you that in death to believe in you is to live again and that in life to believe in you is never to die. Amen.

I have said these things to you so that my joy may be in you, and that your joy may be complete.

John 15:11

7 The Way, the Truth, the Life

As we travel through life, we need to know the way, the way to jobs we shall pursue, the way to values we shall hold, and the way to friends we shall have. It's not easy finding our way in a world like ours. Some jobs aren't worthwhile, some values are fairly shallow, some friends are unhelpful. When Jesus says, *I am the way, and the truth, and the life*, he identifies the true and living way.

Key Text

I am the way, and the truth, and the life.
No one comes to the Father except through me.
If you know me, you will know my Father also.
From now on you do know him and have seen him.
(John 14:6-7)

Context of Key Text in John 14:4-14: 'Jesus the Way to the Father'

In John 13-17 Jesus is preparing his disciples for his coming departure. They will have to face life beyond his death (John 18- 19) and resurrection (John 20-21). The statement of Jesus about *the way, and the truth, and the life* is in response to the question of Thomas, *Lord, we do not know where you are going. How can we know the way?(John 14:5)* In this context Jesus gives purpose in the present and hope for the future.

Content of Key Text

Detail *I am the way, and the truth, and the life.* Jesus is saying that he is the way to God. Life is going somewhere. God is the destination. Jesus is the pathway that leads to God. Jesus is the gateway which opens to the Creator and the Sustainer of the universe and the Saviour and the Restorer of the world. He is the means of access to the meaning of existence. As Jesus said previously, *I am the gate. Whoever enters by me will be saved, and will come in and go out and find pasture.(John 10:9)*

Jesus is saying that he is the way because he is the truth. For the Jew truth meant fidelity. For the Greek truth meant reality. Jesus is the truth in both senses. He is faithful. He is real. He is truth. At his trial the Roman governor asked him, *What is truth?(John 18:38)* Unfortunately, truth was staring Pilate in the face and he didn't recognise it, or I should say, him. Jesus not only gives the revelation which is truth, he is it, the truth in person.

Jesus is saying that he is the way because he is the truth and because he is the life. Jesus is the life of God in our midst. He brings the light of God into the darkness of our world and the darkness cannot put out the light. As it says at the beginning of the Fourth Gospel, *In him was life, and the life was the light of all people. The light shines in the darkness, and the darkness did not overcome it. (John 1:4-5)* Jesus himself talked about this elsewhere, *The thief comes only to steal and kill and destroy. I came that they may have life, and have it abundantly. (John 10:10)*

No one comes to the Father except through me. There is no access to God as Father independent of Jesus. According to a great medieval Christian thinker,

> Without the way, no journey can be taken.
> Without the truth, no truth can be known.
> Without the life, no life can be lived.
> Jesus is the Way which must be followed.
> Jesus is the Truth which must be believed.
> Jesus is the Life which must be lived.

The follower of Jesus is obligated to go the same way that Jesus went: the way of humility, service, and the cross. An example is a schoolteacher named Ellen Arnold. She went as a missionary from Adelaide to Bengal. She worked in Faridpur, Mymensingh, Pabna, Bera, and Ataikola from 1882 to 1931. Her gravestone in Bangladesh bears the Bengali inscription: 'Jesus said, "I am the Way, the Truth, and the Life." Ellen Arnold walked this Way, taught this Truth, and lived this Life.'

In the light of all this, there is a promise. *If you know me, you will know my Father also. From now on you do know him and have seen him.* Knowing Jesus is knowing God. In John's Gospel two verbs for 'know' occur 56 and 85 times. The Gospel is conveying information about Jesus. Also in John's Gospel is another verb which appears 96 times. It's the word for 'believe'. The Gospel is conveying information about Jesus so that we can become personally acquainted with him. John's Gospel wants to change God from someone we know about to someone we come to know in Jesus.

Summary Jesus is the way because he is the pathway that leads to God. He is the means of access to the meaning of existence. Jesus is the way because he is the truth. When we know him, we know the Father. When we see him, we see the Father. Jesus is the way because he is the life. Jesus is the life of God in our midst. He brings God's light into our darkness. The way of humility, the way of service, the way of the cross awaited Jesus and await us. This is what John's Gospel wants us to read and know and believe!

Connections

(a) We are told publicly and privately: 'This is the way to go!' and 'Here is the truth to believe!' and 'That is the life to live!' We are challenged to sort out such claims day by day.
* What do the words 'way', 'truth', and 'life' bring to mind?
(b) The word 'Father' has positive associations for members of a healthy functional family in which parents care for each other, share common interests, and love their children. Otherwise the word has negative associations in dysfunctional families where there is a lack of trust, thoughtfulness, and faithfulness.
* What difference does calling God 'Father' make in our lives?
(c) Our world includes a range of religious options: Hinduism, Buddhism, Judaism, Christianity, Islam, and Atheism.
* How do we answer the claim that every way to God is fine?

Time for Prayer

Guide us lest we wander away from you, Lord Jesus, because you are the way. Help us to trust you, because you are the truth. Assist us to depend only on you, because you are the life. Amen.

8 The True Vine

When people visit Adelaide, they tend to go north to the Barossa Valley or south to McLaren Vale if they enjoy the fruit of the vine. The areas are notable for their spacious vineyards and wineries. Indeed, the South Australian climate is most conducive to fruit growing and vegetable plots in Adelaide. Even an inept gardener like me has enjoyed fruit trees growing in the back yard. We learn the right time to plant, to water, to fertilise, to gather the fruit, and to prune the trees. I think that Jesus, who was once confused with a gardener on a significant occasion, must have known a good deal about gardening.

Key Text

I am the true vine, and my Father is the vine-grower.
He removes every branch in me that bears no fruit.
Every branch that bears fruit he prunes to make it bear more fruit
... I am the vine, you are the branches.
Those who abide in me and I in them bear much fruit, because
apart from me you can do nothing.
(John 15:1-2, 5)

Context of Key Text in John 15:1-17: 'Jesus the True Vine'

Jesus is preparing his disciples in John 13-17 for his coming departure. They will have to face life beyond his death (John 18-19) and resurrection (John 20-21). The statement of Jesus about *the true vine* is in the context of two commands: *Abide in me* (John 15:1-8) and *Abide in my love* (John 15:9-17). Overall the passage makes the point that abiding in Christ and his love bears fruit.

Content of Key Text

Detail The vine is a symbol of the ancient people of God, who had failed to be fruitful. For example, Isaiah of Jerusalem says, *For the vineyard of the LORD of hosts is the house of Israel, and the people of Judah are his pleasant planting; he expected justice, but saw bloodshed; righteousness, but heard a cry!(Isaiah 5:7)* According to Jesus, the ancient people of God still fails to be fruitful. For instance, in the parable of the wicked tenants he says, *What then will the owner of the vineyard do? He will come and destroy the tenants and give the vineyard to others.(Mark 12:9)*

In the time of Jesus there was a great golden vine carved over the gate of the Temple, but all of the Temple was destroyed in AD 70. At the end of Jesus' life, there is the fruit of the vine on the table at the Last Supper, and on the third day the dead Christ becomes the living Lord. The failed vine of the ancient people of God gives way to the successful vine of the people of God, Jew and Gentile, who abide in Jesus.

Jesus is the whole vine, the fruitful vine, with his branches, Jews and Greeks, who abide in him. *I am the true vine, and my Father is the vine-grower.* Jesus promises to cut off dead branches and to cut clean living branches. Jesus promises much fruit. *He removes every branch in me that bears no fruit. Every branch that bears fruit he **prunes** to make it bear more fruit.* And he continues: *You have already been **cleansed** by the word that I have spoken to you.(John 15:3)* There is a play on words *prunes ... cleansed* which is captured by the marginal note of the NRSV: 'The same Greek root refers to pruning and cleansing.'

The disciples are the branches, part of the vine. *I am the vine, you are the branches.* They must abide in Jesus by faith. Then they will bear much fruit. *Those who abide in me and I in them bear much fruit, because apart from me you can do nothing.* The disciples also abide in the words of Jesus and the love of God. Then they will experience much joy. *I have said these things to you so that my joy may be in you, and that your joy may be complete.(John 15:11)*

Abide is a word which occurs often in John's Gospel. It can be translated 'remain' or 'stay' or 'dwell'. To abide in Jesus and his love is the believer's basic duty. It is the thing that constitutes truly Christian life. In Christ alone can Christians live. In him alone there is truly fruitful service to God. In him alone there is answered prayer. In him alone there is loving obedience. Those who abide in him are his friends. And if they belong to him then they are united with each other in his love.

Summary The vine is a symbol of the ancient people of God. According to Jesus, the ancient people of God still fails to be fruitful. Jesus is the whole vine, the fruitful vine, with his branches, Jews and Greeks, who abide in him. Jesus promises to cut off dead branches and to cut clean living branches. Jesus promises much fruit. The disciples are the branches, part of the vine. They must abide in Jesus by faith. Then they will bear much fruit. The disciples also abide in the words of Jesus and the love of God. Then they will experience much joy.

Connections

(a) An ancient Jewish prayer gives thanks for wine: 'Blessed are You, Lord, our God, King of the Universe, who creates the fruit of the vine.' In addition, a second century Christian prayer gives thanks for the cup at the Lord's Supper: 'We thank you, our Father, for the holy vine of David, your child, which you have revealed through Jesus, your child. To you be glory for ever.'

* What associations do vines, vine-growers, and branches have?

(b) Glenn Hinson has suggested that a contemplative lifestyle includes three turnings:

Turn on to God's presence in nature and in our neighbour.
Turn in by meditating on the Bible to find the mind of Christ.
Turn over by surrendering our lives to God.

* How do believers abide in Christ?

(c) In AD 155 the Bishop of Smyrna, Polycarp, died as a martyr because he refused the command of the Roman governor to curse Christ and to pledge his allegiance to Caesar. The response of Polycarp was succinct, 'Eighty-six years I have served him, and he never did me any wrong. How can I blaspheme my King who saved me?' Polycarp exercised widespread influence during his lifetime. His very name is Greek for 'Much Fruit'.

* What 'fruit' results from abiding in Christ?

Time for Prayer

Lord, help us to abide in you so that we may bear the fruits of true service, answered prayer, and loving obedience. Lord, thank you for being our friend and for uniting us in love. Amen.

9 The Night Breeze

Long ago a group of young students heard a tape recording of a sermon by Professor James S. Stewart, in which he said, 'Listen to the wind, Nicodemus! Listen to the wind! You can hear its sound - the night is full of it, hark to it in the tops of the trees -but where it has come from and where it is going no-one knows.' The sermon was based on the conversation in John 3. The impact of Stewart's exposition of the words of Jesus remains fresh to this day.

Key Text

The wind blows where it chooses,
and you hear the sound of it,
but you do not know where it comes from or where it goes.
So it is with everyone who is born of the Spirit.
(John 3:8)

Context of Key Text in John 3:1-21: 'Nicodemus visits Jesus'

The first half of John 3 features an encounter between Jesus and a sympathetic seeker after mature faith named Nicodemus. A dialogue between the two (John 3:1-15) is followed by a monologue by the writer of the Gospel (John 3:16-21). The dialogue is between Jesus, *a teacher who has come from God (John 3:2)*, and Nicodemus, *the teacher of Israel (John 3:10)*. The monologue highlights the significance of *the only Son of God (John 3:18)*.

Content of Key Text

Detail   The speaker is Jesus, the one of whom John the Baptist testifies, *I saw the Spirit descending from heaven like a dove, and it remained on him.(John 1:32)* Jesus talks about the kingdom of God with a Pharisee named Nicodemus, the one to whom Jesus asked, *Are you a [literally, the] teacher of Israel, and yet you do not understand these things?(John 3:10)* Jesus explains entering God's rule and receiving God's kind of life.

Jesus had told a parable of the seed growing secretly with the idea of spontaneous and mysterious natural processes: *the seed would sprout and grow, he does not know how.(Mark 4:27)* He now tells a parable of the night breeze: *The wind blows where it chooses, and you hear the sound of it, but you do not know where it comes from or where it goes.* Both parables are about the coming and growth of God's rule.

There is a play on words: the same word means wind and spirit. On the one hand, it could be translated: The wind blows where it wants, and you hear its sound, but you do not know where it comes from or where it goes. On the other hand, it could be translated: The Spirit breathes where he wills, and you hear his voice, but you do not know where he comes from or where he goes.

Each translation taken by itself is wrong. The point of John's Greek is that Jesus means both wind and spirit. It is hard to reproduce the double meaning in English. The Spirit, like the wind, is wholly beyond human control and comprehension. The Spirit, the wind of God, breathes into this world from God. People themselves cannot fathom the operation of the Spirit, the wind of God, but the Spirit is able to bring people within the sphere of his activity and impart his properties to them.

Jesus is saying to the astonished Nicodemus that salvation is humanly impossible but divinely possible. Salvation means new life in Christ. This is a case of transformation, not just information. *So it is with everyone who is born of the Spirit.* God alone is the source of the Spirit through Jesus. Followers of Jesus can begin to live all over again by the personal power of the Spirit from above. If the wind is real and powerful, so is God's wind, the Spirit, who gives us God's kind of life when we put our trust in Jesus. There are both natural and spiritual processes which are spontaneous and mysterious.

Christianity is not only something to be discussed but it is also something to be experienced. Jesus challenges us not to wait till we know the source of the wind of the Spirit before we let the Spirit refresh and renew us. Jesus encourages us not to wait till we know the destination of the wind of the Spirit before we set our sails on life's ocean. The Spirit empowers believers in Jesus.

Summary Jesus talks about the kingdom of God with a Pharisee named Nicodemus. Jesus explains entering God's rule and receiving God's kind of life. The point of John's Greek is that Jesus means both wind and spirit. Jesus is saying that salvation is humanly impossible but divinely possible. If the wind is real and powerful so is God's wind, the Spirit, who gives us God's kind of life by faith. The Spirit empowers believers in Jesus.

Connections

(a) Change can be a painful process. Shock and disbelief, feelings of insecurity, physical symptoms, feelings of guilt and panic, outbursts of anger and frustration, and idealisation of the past can be negative features for someone who is reluctant to change. However, on the long road of change there are positive features of realism, attitude, acceptance, and action.
* Why do some people stubbornly resist a personal transformation like Nicodemus?
(b) William Barclay tells the story of a drunken and immoral worker who was converted to Christ. His workmates made life hard for him. They asked him, 'Surely you can't believe in miracles. You really don't believe that Jesus turned water into wine, do you?' He replied, 'I don't know whether Jesus turned water into wine when he was in Palestine, but I do know that in my home he has turned beer into furniture!'
* How can habits of a lifetime be changed in a time of decision?
(c) Over a century ago William James identified conversion as a gradual or sudden process by which a divided self, consciously wrong, inferior, and unhappy became consciously right, superior, and happy as a result of a firmer grasp of religious realities.
* Is a new start possible apart from Jesus' life and message?

Time for Prayer

Lord, let the Spirit of Jesus bring your changing power into our lives as we believe. Thank you for opportunities to serve you and help us to make the most of these opportunities. Amen.

10 The Bridegroom and the Best Man

There is an old joke that is told at weddings. People will say that the best man did not get the bride. Of course, this is a play on words. 'Best man' is the way we refer to the chief attendant of the bridegroom at a wedding. In another context 'best man' can mean the best man for a job or a position. In the time of Jesus the best man arranged the wedding feast, brought the bride to the bridegroom's house, and acted as a guard of the couple on their wedding night.

Key Text

He who has the bride is the bridegroom.
The friend of the bridegroom,
who stands and hears him,
rejoices greatly at the bridegroom's voice.
(John 3:29)

Context of Key Text in John 3:25-36: 'Jesus and John the Baptist'

The second half of John 3 features a dialogue between John the Baptist and his followers (John 3:25-30) and a monologue by the writer of the Gospel (John 3:31-36). The dialogue is about Jesus, the one to whom John the Baptist had testified, the one who is baptizing, and the one to whom all are going. John recalls that he said, *I am not the Messiah, but I have been sent ahead of him.(John 3:28)* The monologue highlights the importance of Jesus who *speaks the words of God* and to whom God *gives the Spirit without measure.(John 3:34)*

Content of Key Text

Detail The speaker is John the Baptist who had come before Jesus. John is aware that he had prepared the way for Jesus. He is being asked about the success of Jesus. John answers with a parable of a wedding. He makes a comparison between the bridegroom and the best man.

Elsewhere Jesus speaks in terms of a wedding. *The wedding guests cannot fast while the bridegroom is with them, can they? As long as they have the bridegroom with them, they cannot fast. The days will come when the bridegroom is taken away from them, and then they will fast on that day.(Mark 2:19-20)* In the Old Testament God is pictured as the husband of his people. For example, *I will take you for my wife in righteousness and in justice, in steadfast love, and in mercy. (Hosea 2:19)* In time the idea of the Messiah as the coming bridegroom of God's people developed naturally.

John the Baptist himself uses a genuine picture from real life to portray the coming Messiah as a harvester whose *winnowing fork is in his hand, and he will clear his threshing floor and will gather his wheat into the granary; but the chaff he will burn with unquenchable fire.(Matthew 3:12)*

So, in another genuine picture from real life John the Baptist portrays Jesus as the coming Messiah, *the bridegroom*, God's chosen people as *the bride*, and himself as the supporting act, *the friend of the bridegroom*, the best man. *He who has the bride is the bridegroom. The friend of the bridegroom, who stands and hears him, rejoices greatly at the bridegroom's voice.*

One is reminded of the vision of another John, the seer of Patmos, the vision of a marriage of the messianic bridegroom and his bride. The bride of the Messiah portrays a new people and a new city, in a new heaven and a new earth: *The marriage of the Lamb has come, and his bride has made herself ready (Revelation 19:7)* and *I saw the holy city, the new Jerusalem, coming down out of heaven from God, prepared as a bride adorned for her husband. (Revelation 21:2)*

At a wedding the best man gladly supports and gives way joyfully to the bridegroom so that attention is focussed on the bridegroom and his bride. Similarly, John the Baptist, having prepared the way for Jesus the Messiah, fades painlessly into the background. The one who said, *Here is the Lamb of God who takes away the sin of the world!* and *I saw the Spirit descending from heaven like a dove, and it remained on him (John 1:29, 32)*, now says, *He must increase, but I must decrease. (John 3:30)*

John the Baptist gladly gives way to Jesus the Messiah, who brings us God's Spirit. John is happy to be a servant who has no wish to displace his master. This lesson never goes out of date.

Summary The Baptist is being asked about the success of Jesus. He makes a comparison between a bridegroom and a best man. In the Old Testament God was pictured as the husband of his people. In time the idea of the Messiah as the coming bridegroom of God's people developed naturally. John portrays Jesus as the coming Messiah, *the bridegroom*, God's chosen people as *the bride*, and himself as the supporting act, *the friend of the bridegroom*, the best man. The Baptist gladly gives way to Jesus the Messiah, who brings us God's Spirit.

Connections

(a) The Baptist prepares the way for Jesus. In the story of Jesus different characters have to learn, as C.S. Lewis once wrote, 'to play great parts without pride and small parts without shame'. Sometimes in church life we seek to play a major role with pride and we are tempted to play a minor role with shame.
* How can the danger of religious jealousy be avoided between followers of Jesus?

(b) The Baptist's actions are congruent with his words. He is praised for directing people's attention to the life and teaching of Jesus. How different is the following statement of a well known philosopher to a colleague: 'Your actions speak so loud that I cannot hear what you are saying.'
* How can we be like John the Baptist and insure that people see and hear Jesus through us?

(c) Jesus in his time and place was one among a variety of possible religious and political leaders such as the Sadducees, the Pharisees, the Essenes, and the Zealots. This is even more so in our time and place. We can think of Christian and non-Christian, secular and sacred leaders.
*How and why is Jesus superior to other religious and political leaders?

Time for Prayer

Lord, help us to be humble witnesses to Jesus like John the Baptist. Let our words and deeds point towards Jesus. Assist us to avoid making ourselves the focus of attention. Amen.

11 The Ripe Fields

What is the difference between a pessimist and an optimist at a sports stadium? Is it that a pessimist sees a stadium partly empty and an optimist sees a stadium partly full? A rather cynical writer has said, 'The optimist proclaims that we live in the best of all possible worlds; and the pessimist fears this is true.' Was Jesus a realistic optimist?

Key Text

Do you not say,'Four months more, then comes the harvest'?
But I tell you, look around you,
and see how the fields are ripe for harvesting.
The reaper is already receiving wages and is gathering fruit
for eternal life, so that sower and reaper may rejoice together.
For here the saying holds true,'One sows and another reaps.'
I sent you to reap that for which you did not labour.
Others have laboured, and you have entered into their labour.
(John 4:35-38)

Context of Key Text in John 4:31-42: 'Jesus and the Woman of Samaria'

In John 4 Jesus breaks down three barriers: ethnic in verse 9b (*Jews do not share things in common with Samaritans*), religious in verse 20 (*Our ancestors worshipped on this mountain, but you say that the place where people must worship is in Jerusalem*), and sexual in verse 27 (*his disciples ... were astonished that he was speaking with a woman*). So it is that the disciples are challenged (John 4:31-38) and the Samaritans are converted (John 4:39-42).

Content of Key Text

Detail   The Samaritans expected a Coming One whom they called Taheb, the Restorer. In the narrative a Samaritan woman makes the link between the Samaritans' Taheb and the Jews' Messiah. *I know that Messiah is coming ... When he comes, he will proclaim all things to us.(John 4:25)*

After the dialogue of Jesus with the Samaritan woman the parable of the ripe fields is told by Jesus on the return of the disciples from the nearby town. Jesus seeks to teach the disciples that he is active in the work of his messengers. He had used the same word picture elsewhere. *The harvest is plentiful, but the labourers are few; therefore ask the Lord of the harvest to send out labourers into his harvest.(Matthew 9:37-38)*

Jesus tells the disciples, *I tell you, look around you, and see how the fields are ripe for harvesting.* Jesus is challenging the disciples to lift up their eyes and see the Samaritans coming from the town. The strangers are fulfilling Jesus' words: *the hour is coming, and is now here, when the true worshippers will worship the Father in spirit and truth.(John 4:23)*

Jesus says, *The reaper is already receiving wages and is gathering fruit for eternal life.* The reaper of the harvest is being rewarded with fruit not for a passing season but for life in the messianic age. The harvest is taking place. The reaper is overtaking the sower. The prophets, John the Baptist, and Jesus had sowed, the disciples now reap. *For here the saying holds true, 'One sows and another reaps.'* The promises of the messianic age are coming true for the followers of Jesus.

I sent you to reap that for which you did not labour. Others have laboured, and you have entered into their labour. The past tense *I sent* is spoken in anticipation with prophetic assurance. Jesus treats the future as already present. The disciples are learning that they are links in the chain stretching from the patriarchs (Abraham, Isaac, Jacob) to the parousia (the second coming of Jesus).

Finally, the experience of the Samaritans' faith grows out of the effective witness of the Samaritan woman to Jesus. They acknowledge, *It is no longer because of what you said that we believe, for we have heard for ourselves, and we know that this is truly the Saviour of the world.(John 4:42)* Second hand hearers of God's message through the woman become first hand hearers through Jesus, God's message in person.

The account of Jesus and the Samaritans in John 4:1-42 foreshadows the Samaritan mission of Philip, Peter and John in Acts 8:4-25. Philip goes to Samaria, proclaims the Messiah, and people receive the message joyfully. Peter and John represent Jerusalem followers of Jesus and give the stamp of approval to a Samaritan Pentecost.

Summary Jesus seeks to teach the disciples that he is active in the work of his messengers. Jesus is challenging the disciples to lift up their eyes and see the Samaritans coming from the town. The harvest is taking place. The reaper is overtaking the sower. The promises of the messianic age are coming true for the followers of Jesus. Jesus treats the future as already present. Jesus and the Samaritans in John 4 foreshadow the apostles and the Samaritans in Acts 8.

Connections

(a) The disciples are thinking of their lunch: '*Rabbi, eat something.*' ... '*Surely no one has brought him something to eat?*' *(John 4:31, 33)* But Jesus is thinking of his vocation: '*I have food to eat that you do not know about.*' ... '*My food is to do the will of him who sent me and to complete his work.*' *(John 4:32, 34)*

* Are there times when we miss the point of Jesus' words?

(b) In the 1930s H.V. Morton wrote of his visit to Samaria: 'But as I sat by Jacob's Well a crowd of Arabs came along the road from the direction in which Jesus was looking, and I saw their white garments shining in the sun. Surely Jesus was speaking not of the earthly but of the heavenly harvest, and as He spoke I think it likely that He pointed along the road where the Samaritans in their white robes were assembling to hear His words.'

* How does the picture of the ripe fields encourage followers of Jesus?

(c) In church groups there are people with various talents to contribute and various tasks to perform in a range of activities. Activities are designed for maintenance and/or mission. Upfront leaders come and go to a greater extent than regular members.

* As sowers or reapers how do we rejoice with fellow believers in sharing the message of Jesus?

Time for Prayer

Lord, give us not just sight but insight as we consider the words and deeds of Jesus. Let us rejoice with fellow believers in sharing the gift of eternal life with other people. Amen.

12 The Apprentice Son

Frederick Buechner makes a wise observation about finding the work that God wants us to do. 'The kind of work God usually calls you to is the kind of work (a) that you most need to do and (b) that the world most needs to have done.' The parable of the apprentice son implies that Jesus faced this challenge too.

Key Text

Very truly, I tell you, the Son can do nothing on his own,
but only what he sees the Father doing;
for whatever the Father does, the Son does likewise.
The Father loves the Son
and shows him all that he himself is doing ...
(John 5:19-20a)

Context of Key Text in John 5:19-30: 'The Authority of the Son'

In John 5:1-9a Jesus cures a lame man on the sabbath at the Pool of Bethesda, which means 'House of Divine Mercy' in Hebrew. Bethzatha is the Aramaic equivalent. As a result, Jesus is criticised by Jewish religious leaders (John 5:9b-18). He makes claims as the Son of the Father that he can give life and exercise judgment (John 5:19-30). Finally, he gives evidence for the claims (John 5:31-47).

Content of Key Text

Detail   After being criticised for healing on the sabbath, Jesus links his work with God's work of creation. *My Father is* *still working, and I also am working.(John 5:17)* The Jewish religious leaders are furious because he makes himself equal with the Creator and puts himself beyond their jurisdiction.

He continues to discuss his relationship with God by telling the parable of the apprentice son. He equates his work with God's work. He sees himself not acting on his own because everything he does is modelled on what God does. As Jesus said elsewhere, *And no one knows the Son except the Father, and no one knows the Father except the Son (Matthew 11:27).* Only the Father and the Son really know each other.

The parable begins with *Very truly*, literally, *Amen, amen.* Normally the word Amen is used at the end of a solemn statement as in prayer. Jesus uses it at the beginning of an important statement and he doubles its use. Jesus is making a solemn declaration. According to the Gospel writer, the relationship between the Son and the Father in our key text is like the relationship between the Word and God. *In the beginning was the Word, and the Word was with God, and the Word was God. He was in the beginning with God. All things came into being through him. And without him not one thing came into being that has come into being. (John 1:1-3)*

Jesus is employing a simple picture of a son apprenticed to his father's trade. Perhaps he remembers his time in the carpenter's shop at Nazareth with his earthly father Joseph. After all, he was called *the carpenter's son (Matthew 13:55)*. Jesus is transforming and deepening a simple picture.

Negatively, *the Son can do nothing on his own, but only what he sees the Father doing.* Jesus as a young man in the carpenter's shop would have been an apprentice learning from the example of Joseph.

Positively, *for whatever the Father does, the Son does likewise.* Jesus as a young apprentice would have imitated the techniques and processes of Joseph in the family business.

By way of explanation, Jesus says, *The Father loves the Son and shows him all that he himself is doing.* Joseph as a human father would have been known as a just and caring person who loved the mother of Jesus and their children. Thus the parable of the apprentice son points toward unity of action between Jesus and God and complete dependence of the Son on the Father.

Indeed, John 5:19-30 answers two questions in two tenses. The question 'Who is Jesus?' receives an answer. Jesus shares the power of life and judgment with God in the present (verses 19-23) and in the future (verses 26-27). The question 'What are people in response to Jesus?' also receives an answer. People can hear, believe, and pass from death to life in the present (verses 24-25). In the future all people will be raised, some to life, others to condemnation (verses 28-29).

Summary After being criticised for healing on the sabbath, Jesus links his work with God's work of creation. He continues to discuss his relationship with God by telling the parable of the apprentice son. Jesus as a young apprentice in the carpenter's shop would have learned from, imitated, and appreciated Joseph. The parable of the apprentice son points toward unity of action between Jesus and God and complete dependence of the Son on the Father. The parable and the words that follow challenge us to believe.

Connections

(a) In every day life we often say, 'Like father, like son' or 'Like mother, like daughter'. I remember a mother wondering aloud why her children were so independent. A friend advised her to look at their parents!
* What are some things which we remember our parents doing and today find ourselves doing?
(b) In previous times it was quite common for a son to follow in his father's trade or profession. One thinks of a plumbing business founded by a competent tradesman, passed down to son, and then grandson. Each generation won renown for honest work.
* What tasks does Jesus say that he shares with his Father?
(c) In John 5 Jesus was criticised for claiming to share with God the right to work on the day of rest and worship. By way of reply Jesus implied that he acted in union with God and with complete dependence on God.
* As criticism sharpened Jesus' self-understanding, has criticism helped us evaluate our work's motivation and effectiveness?

Time for Prayer

Lord, help us, as we mature, to imitate the strengths but not the weaknesses of our parents and, as we face criticisms, to evaluate our performance of tasks honestly. Amen.

13 The Slave and the Son

Kierkegaard criticised the church of his day in a parable. Farmyard geese went to church each week. The goose preacher would talk about the Creator Goose who had made them to fly. But the talk of flying was not taken seriously with one exception. The geese were too fat to fly. However, one goose tried to fly and was viewed by the others as weird. Indeed, he succeeded, flew into the sky, and returned to tell everyone about it. But he was ignored. Every Sunday all the geese went to church to hear the same message. They said, 'Amen!' and waddled home. Finally, all the geese were cooked for Christmas dinner, except for the goose who had learned to fly! The parable can be taken as an illustration of the difference between the slave and the son in Jesus' parable according to John.

Key Text

The slave does not have a permanent place in the household; the son has a place there for ever.
(John 8:35)

Context of Key Text in John 8:31-38: 'True Disciples'

John 8 is about Jesus as the judge of life. The chapter features the consequence of believing and obeying Jesus. Jesus is in the Temple and is speaking to people who have started to believe but are not necessarily going to continue. If they do continue to hold to his message, then they will continue in the household of God. If they truly change their understanding of Jesus, then they will change their understanding of themselves.

Content of Key Text

Detail   Jesus is saying that a slave is not a permanent member of the household, but a son is a permanent member. His hearers claim to have never been slaves to anyone. They conveniently overlook their ancestors in slavery to Egypt and their contemporaries in servitude to Rome.

Slaves were a common feature in the Roman world. They were an indispensable part of the empire's economy. They were subordinate to and dominated by their masters and suffered harsh punishment, brutal torture, and virulent abuse. Sons, on the other hand, were highly valued. They continued the family name and maintained possession of the family inheritance.

The contrast between a slave and a son is evident in the story of Abraham in Genesis 21. Ishmael, the slave son of Hagar the slave girl, is deemed inferior to Isaac, the free son of Sarah.

The contrast is also seen in an intricate interpretation of Genesis 21 by Paul in Galatians 4. People who misunderstand the purpose of the law at Sinai belong to the earthly Jerusalem, in a human covenant, like the child of the slave woman. People who rightly understand the promise of God through Abraham belong to the heavenly Jerusalem, in a divine covenant, like the child of the free woman.

In John 8 Jesus is contrasting the slave and the son. *The slave does not have a permanent place in the household; the son has a place there for ever.* Whereas a slave does not remain permanently in a household a son does. The point is well made. Followers of Jesus possess the privilege of being sons and daughters of God. They can rest secure in the knowledge of the care of the heavenly Father.

Next, Jesus contrasts the slave and the ex-slave. *So if the Son makes you free, you will be free indeed.(John 8:36)* The ex-slave is the one whom Jesus, the Son of God, sets free. Only the Son of God can make the slave into a son or daughter of God through believing in Jesus.

What a difference Jesus makes in the life of a believer! He gives the forgiven sinner a revitalising relationship with God, an abiding inheritance among God's people, and a liberating freedom to face the future with Christ.

One is reminded of the words of Paul: *There is no longer Jew or Greek, there is no longer slave or free, there is no longer male and female; for all of you are one in Christ Jesus. (Galatians 3:28)*

Summary In Roman times slaves tended to be treated as things, sons were highly valued. Jews knew the contrast between Ishmael, the slave son of Hagar, and Isaac, the free son of Sarah. Followers of Jesus possess the privilege of being not like a slave but like a son. Only the Son of God can make a slave into a son or daughter of God.

Connections

(a) Slavery was not formally abolished until 1833 in the British Empire and 1865 in the United States. Yet it continues in other guises such as enforcement of child labour and second class treatment of women in various countries throughout the world.

* What would it be like to be a slave in ancient and modern times?

(b) Parallels to the distinction between a slave in a household and a child in a family exist today. Sometimes the favouritism of parents can be apparent in a family. One child can be treated as important and another as unimportant. At times the treatment and mistreatment of employees can be obvious in a workplace. Workers can be treated as slaves.

* What are the differences between being a slave in a household and a favoured child in a family?

(c) Human personality can provide extreme examples. Some people are cases of 'all talk and no action'. Other people are cases of 'actions speak louder than words'. Are we people of word and/or deed as we seek to follow Jesus? Do we live as highly valued children of God?

* What are we meant to be and do as human beings in response to Jesus?

Time for Prayer

Lord, we thank you for the opportunity to respond to Jesus and to be children of God. Help us to trust ourselves to the care of our heavenly Father in all that life brings. Amen.

14 The Shepherd and the Stranger

In the Australian outback a utility truck takes the sheep farmer with his sheep dogs to round up large flocks of sheep. The sheep are carted to the wool sheds for shearing or to the abattoirs for butchering. How different were Bible times! A shepherd kept his small flock in a sheepfold near his cottage for their milk and wool. Outside the sheepfold the shepherd went in front of them and called them by name. The sheep followed the shepherd but they would not follow a stranger.

Key Text

Very truly, I tell you,
anyone who does not enter the sheepfold by the gate
but climbs in by another way is a thief and a bandit.
The one who enters by the gate is the shepherd of the sheep.
The gatekeeper opens the gate for him,
and the sheep hear his voice.
He calls his own sheep by name and leads them out.
When he has brought out all his own, he goes ahead of them,
and the sheep follow him because they know his voice.
They will not follow a stranger, but they will run from him
because they do not know the voice of strangers.
(John 10:1-5)

Context of Key Text in John 10:1-21: 'The Shepherd of Life'

The first half of John 10 is about Jesus as the shepherd of life. Jesus uses a figure of speech about the shepherd, the thief, and the doorkeeper to make his hearers think (John 10:1-6). Jesus explains himself in two ways. He uses the symbols of the gate, or the door, (John 10:7-10) and the good shepherd (John 10:11-18). The section closes with division about his words (John 10:19-21) just as there had previously been division about his miraculous healing of a man born blind (John 9:39-41).

Content of Key Text

Detail Once again Jesus begins with *Very truly*, literally, *Amen, amen.* As we have seen, the word Amen is usually at the end of a prayer. By using it twice at the beginning of a statement Jesus indicates the solemnity of his declaration. He describes the difference between the thief or bandit and the shepherd.

The danger of *a thief and a bandit* who enters a sheepfold illegally probably refers to the dishonesty and violence of religious leaders who oppose Jesus and his followers. For example, the authorities in John 9 refused to acknowledge the reality of the healing by Jesus of the man born blind and treated the man harshly and unfairly.

On the other hand, *the shepherd of the sheep* recalls two types of references. In the Old Testament God himself replaces treacherous leaders and says, *I myself will be the shepherd of my sheep ... I will set up over them one shepherd, my servant David.(Ezekiel 34:15, 23)* In the New Testament it is said of Jesus: *When he saw the crowds, he had compassion for them, because they were harassed and helpless, like sheep without a shepherd.(Matthew 9:36)*

It is likely that *the sheepfold* and *the gatekeeper* are just parts of the figure of speech, not parts of the developed symbolism. The gatekeeper admits the rightful entrant to the sheepfold. (The symbols of the gate and the shepherd are explained in the 'I am' sayings which follow in John 10:7-18.)

Of course, *the sheep* are the people of God. They recognise the shepherd's voice. The shepherd calls his sheep by name. The shepherd also leads them to safe pasture. The sheep follow their shepherd, but *will not follow a stranger* who is to be equated with *a thief and a bandit*.

In the 1930s H.V. Morton described a scene near Bethlehem. 'Two shepherds had evidently spent the night with their flocks in a cave. The sheep were all mixed together and the time had come for the shepherds to go in different directions. One of the shepherds stood some distance from the sheep and began to call. First one, then another, then four or five animals ran towards him; and so on until he had counted his whole flock.'

The words of our key text came to Morton's mind. *He calls his own sheep by name and leads them out ... and the sheep follow him because they know his voice.* Jesus is no thief, no bandit, no stranger. He is the true shepherd who gathers, guards, and guides.

Summary Jesus describes the difference between the stranger and the shepherd. Dishonest and violent religious leaders oppose Jesus and his followers. The true shepherd is God in the Old Testament and Jesus in the New Testament. The sheep are the people of God who recognise the shepherd's voice.

Connections

(a) Today's religions include some good and creative things in health care and education, some evil and vicious things such as 'holy wars', and a very good thing - a concern for our ultimate destiny. Today's religious leaders include the good, the bad, and the visionary.
* Who are the thief, the bandit, and the stranger in our world?
(b) Robert Frost's 1923 poem 'Stopping by Woods on a Snowy Evening' spoke of life's challenges:

> The woods are lovely, dark and deep.
> But I have promises to keep,
> And miles to go before I sleep,
> And miles to go before I sleep.

* What does Jesus the true shepherd promise his followers?
(c) A famous logo on some old records has a dog sitting by an old fashioned gramophone with his head to one side listening to the sound coming out of the trumpet of the gramophone as a record is playing. The record label is HMV, 'His Master's Voice'.
* What is required of the sheep by the true shepherd Jesus?

Time for Prayer

Lord, help us listen to our master's voice. Let us see what is important and what is unimportant, what is true and what is false. Let us follow the true shepherd all our days. Amen.

15 The Traveller in the Dark

It is hard for dwellers in modern urban centres to imagine city life without electricity. Our ancestors faced the night time with candles or lamps. They got up at sunrise, worked by the light of the sun, returned home by sunset, and went to bed early by our standards. The contrast between day and night was all too real. To be a traveller in the dark was a hazardous business.

Key Text

Are there not twelve hours of daylight?
Those who walk during the day do not stumble,
because they see the light of this world.
But those who walk at night stumble,
because the light is not in them.
(John 11:9-10)

Context of Key Text in John 11:7-16: 'The Death of Lazarus'

John 11 is about Jesus the resurrection and the life. It relates the story of the death of Lazarus at Bethany. Before Jesus and his disciples reach the home of Lazarus Jesus tells them the parable of the traveller in the dark. Later on Jesus meets Martha and then Mary, the grieving sisters of Lazarus. Finally, Jesus goes to the tomb of Lazarus and the unexpected happens.

Content of Key Text

Detail In the other Gospels Jesus tells parables of crisis about a rich fool, in Luke 12:16-21, and about sheep and goats, in

Matthew 25:31-46. By means of these parables Jesus teaches that decisions for and against the rule of God are crucial. To follow Jesus is to decide for him in the crises of life and death. Such decisions are of ultimate and eternal consequence.

In John 11 Jesus and the disciples are facing a crisis. Jesus is in danger. When they learn of Lazarus' illness, Jesus asks them to accompany him to the home of Lazarus in Judea. So, at the beginning, the disciples said, *Rabbi, the Jews were just now trying to stone you, and are you going there again? (John 11:8)* At the end, after the unexpected sign of God's power in the raising of Lazarus from the dead, it is said of the religious authorities: *So from that day on they planned to put him* (Jesus) *to death.(John 11:53)*

Jesus tells another parable of crisis, the parable of the traveller in the dark. He begins with a rhetorical question. *Are there not twelve hours of daylight?* Jesus wants to make his listeners think. During the twelve hours of daylight there are the advantages of being safe and seeing the way ahead. Walking securely in the light of day is different from stumbling perilously in the dark. In the time of Jesus movement during daylight hours was free and unhindered, but darkness brought carefree activity to an end.

Those who walk during the day do not stumble, because they see the light of this world. On the one hand, Jesus is the walker by day who does not stumble as the night of his betrayal, arrest, trial, and crucifixion approaches. Jesus must make the most of the short time which still remains of his life. The ministry of Jesus is not over yet. As Jesus had said, *We must work the works of him who sent me while it is day; night is coming when no one can work.(John 9:4)* On the other hand, the followers of Jesus are to be the walkers by day who do not stumble during the night of disloyalty, like Judas the one who betrayed Jesus when *it was night (John 13:30)*, or during the night of persecution, like the disciples behind locked doors for *fear of the Jews (John 20:19)*.

On another occasion Jesus had said, *The eye is the lamp of the body. So, if your eye is healthy, your whole body will be full of light; but if your eye is unhealthy, your whole body will be full of darkness. If then the light in you is darkness, how great is the darkness!(Matthew 6:22-23)* Sound eyesight brings things into focus but unsound eyesight fails to do so. Accordingly, the eye acts as the lamp of the body. It gives the body light or leaves the body in the dark. The healthy eye represents being open to God's message. The unhealthy eye represents being closed to the divine message. The difference is the nature of *the light in you.*

But those who walk at night stumble. If Jesus and his followers failed to walk in the light, then they would be succumbing to the darkness. Instead of walking securely in the light, they would be stumbling over unseen obstacles in the dark. The reason would have been quite simple: *because the light is not in them.*

As Jesus had to use to the full the short time which remained to him on earth, so followers of Jesus have to do God's work in the security of Jesus' presence before the dangers of opposition or death come. Jesus is saying that we should be concerned to use our time well and to beware of travelling in the dark.

Summary Jesus tells a parable of crisis. Jesus is the walker by day who does not stumble as the night of his betrayal, arrest, trial, and crucifixion approaches. The followers of Jesus are to be the walkers by day who don't stumble during the night of disloyalty and persecution. We should be concerned to use our time well and to beware of travelling in the dark.

Connections

(a) An early Christian writer offered the following comment: *This is the message we have heard from him and proclaim to you, that God is light and in him there is no darkness at all.(1 John 1:5)*
* How do we avail ourselves of the light of God?
(b) Today's world offers many examples of darkness in which good things have gone bad. For instance, one may think of the misuse of money, power, and sex.
* What are the forces of darkness that most threaten us today?
(c) An employee's contract was not renewed by his employers. The troubled worker went to his doctor for treatment of symptoms arising from his uncertain situation. The doctor treated the symptoms and also said, 'If I were in your position, I would show them by your performance that they were wrong!' This advice carried the employee through the time remaining.
* What does the key text say to a person in crisis?

Time for Prayer

Lord, help us to do God's work in the security of Jesus' presence before the darkness of opposition or the nearness of death hinders our effective output. Amen.

16 The Grain of Wheat

City folks, and I am one of them, can overlook the processes of the farm and the orchard. We can ignore where the ingredients for our favourite wholemeal bread come from and what the sources of our morning fruit juices happen to be. The grains of wheat are planted and in time produce the golden harvest. The orange pips and apple seeds are buried and in due course become the saplings which grow into healthy fruit trees. Country folks will understand the parable of the grain of wheat.

Key Text

Very truly, I tell you,
unless a grain of wheat falls into the earth and dies,
it remains just a single grain;
but if it dies, it bears much fruit.
(John 12:24)

Context of Key Text in John 12:20-26: 'Some Greeks wish to see Jesus'

John 12 is preparing for the Passover festival at which time Jesus will be arrested, tried, crucified, buried, and raised from death. The first half of the chapter follows a plot against Jesus, mentions his anointing by Mary, a plot against Lazarus, his triumphal entry into Jerusalem, and the request of some Greeks to meet Jesus. The parable of the grain of wheat is his response.

Content of Key Text

Detail   Jesus is facing the consequences of the entry into

Jerusalem on Palm Sunday. Legalistic religious leaders oppose Jesus. But some Greeks on a genuine quest for the truth want to see Jesus. He responds with the parable of the grain of wheat.

This is not the first time that Jesus uses the imagery of nature. The kingdom of God *is like a mustard seed ... the smallest of all the seeds on earth ... becomes the greatest of all shrubs ... so that the birds of the air can make nests in its shade.(Mark 4:31-32)* He compares the productivity of a mustard seed to the coming of Gentiles to God. He also compares the work of a sower to the preacher of God's rule. *Listen! A sower went out to sow ... The sower sows the word.(Mark 4:3, 14)*

In John's Gospel the emphasis moves from the sower to the seed. *Very truly*, literally, *Amen, amen*, indicates the solemnity of the statement. It is generally true that *unless a grain of wheat falls into the earth and dies, it remains just a single grain; but if it dies, it bears much fruit*. But it is specifically true of Jesus. The kingdom of God is concentrated in the person of the king. Jesus is saying pictorially what he will say plainly very soon, *And I, when I am lifted up from the earth, will draw all people to myself.(John 12:32)* The death of Jesus is the costly price for God's kind of life being available to all of us.

Just as we cannot really see the meaning of wheat by looking at a tiny seed until it is buried and grows as a stalk of wheat, so the Greeks cannot really see the meaning of Jesus until he dies and rises again and draws all people to himself through his followers. The parable of the grain of wheat points to the death of Jesus as necessary and fruitful. Through his death and resurrection Jesus will become accessible for the Greeks as the dying and risen Lord.

The meaning of the parable of the grain of wheat is seen in a saying of Jesus when he speaks of his death. *For the Son of Man came not to be served but to serve, and to give his life a ransom for many.(Mark 10:45)* According to Mark, Jesus is explaining his death in four ways: voluntary(*came ... to serve*), costly (*came ... to give his life*), sacrificial (*a ransom*), effective (*for many*).

The influence of the parable of the grain of wheat is evident in Paul's letters when he discusses the mystery of life arising from death at the final resurrection. What is said of Jesus in John 12:24 is said of the followers of Jesus in 1 Corinthians 15:36, *What you sow does not come to life unless it dies.*

The parable is followed by a saying about discipleship. *Those who love their life lose it, and those who hate their life in this world will keep it for eternal life.(John 12:25)* In other words, those who wish to live in and for themselves will be disillusioned. Elsewhere Jesus says, *For those who want to save their life will lose it, and those who lose their life for my sake, and for the sake of the gospel, will save it.(Mark 8:35)* Those who wish to save their skin will be disappointed. We follow Jesus through thick and thin.

Summary In response to negative opposition and positive enquiry Jesus tells the parable of the grain of wheat. It is generally true that without pain there is no gain. But it is specifically true that the death of Jesus is the costly price for God's kind of life being available to all of us. The parable's meaning is seen in Mark 10:45. The parable's influence is evident in 1 Corinthians 15:36. After the parable comes a saying about following Jesus through thick and thin.

Connections

(a) 'Cometh the hour, cometh the man.' Before he tells the parable of the grain of wheat Jesus says, *The hour has come for the Son of Man to be glorified.(John 12:23)*. After Judas goes to betray him and before he goes to his arrest, trial, and death, only then Jesus speaks of his hour of glory (John 13:31-32; 17:1).
* Why does Jesus seem to put off the opportunity presented by the Greeks?
(b) In the second century Tertullian declared, 'The blood of the martyrs is the seed of the Church.' He meant that as often as Christians were put to death for their faith, the more Christians grew in numbers.
* What is the lesson of the contrast between the single grain and much fruit?
(c) William Barclay mentions the attitude of a famous Welsh evangelist, Christmas Evans. His friends would tell him to take life easier and to slow down. But he would say, 'It's better to burn out than to rust out.'
* Who are some people who have followed Christ sacrificially?

Time for Prayer

Lord, we think of the death of Jesus which is the costly price for God's kind of life being available to all of us. Let us learn to be unselfish like Jesus and so by his grace bear much fruit. Amen.

17 The Walker at Sunset

In the big cities of our world there are places where it is advisable not to go alone after dark. The same places are probably secure during the daylight hours. For example, I have walked safely through Central Park in New York City but not at night. Walkers at sunset in such a place would be well advised to get going while the going is good, and not let the darkness overtake them.

Key Text

The light is with you for a little longer.
Walk while you have the light,
so that the darkness may not overtake you.
If you walk in the darkness,
you do not know where you are going.
While you have the light, believe in the light,
so that you may become children of light.
(John 12:35-36)

Context of Key Text in John 12:27-36a: 'Jesus speaks about his death'

John 12 is preparing for the Passover festival at which time Jesus will be arrested, tried, crucified, buried, and raised from death. The second half of the chapter follows the request of some Greeks and the response of Jesus, mentions his commitment to his calling in the face of rejection by the people, and sums up his teaching. The parable of the walker at sunset underlines the commitment of Jesus.

Content of Key Text

Detail   As we noted about the parable of the traveller in the dark, in the other Gospels Jesus tells parables of crisis. Such parables teach that decisions for and against the rule of God are crucial. The saying about the walker at sunset is another parable of crisis.

Jesus is in danger. The religious authorities *had given orders that anyone who knew where Jesus was should let them know, so that they might arrest him.(John 11:57)* Lazarus is in danger. The religious authorities *planned to put Lazarus to death as well, since it was on account of him that many of the Jews were deserting and were believing in Jesus.(John 12:10-11)*

By the time Jesus has entered Jerusalem and has responded to the approach of the Greeks with the parable of the grain of wheat (John 12:24), things are getting very serious. Jesus gives the crowd one last chance to see the light, to recognise the light, to be in the light. He does this by telling the parable of the walker at sunset.

The light is with you for a little longer. Jesus is conscious that his ministry is drawing to a close. He has just spoken about being *lifted up from the earth* indicating *the kind of death he was to die (John 12:32-33).* Jesus is reflecting the description of the Servant of the Lord in the teaching of Isaiah of Babylon. The Servant is *a light to the nations (Isaiah 49:6)*, is to be *lifted up (Isaiah 52:13)*, and is *a man of suffering (Isaiah 53:3).* Jesus, the light of the world, is willing to go to his death. Perhaps Jesus is encouraged by the words of Isaiah of Babylon: *Out of his anguish he shall see light (Isaiah 53:11).*

Jesus compares day and night. *Walk while you have the light, so that the darkness may not overtake you. If you walk in the darkness, you do not know where you are going.* In his ministry Jesus has brought the rays of God's light into a self centred, uncaring, dark world. As the Gospel writer says, *The light shines in the darkness, and the darkness did not overcome it. (John 1:5)* Beyond Jesus' ministry John's Gospel continues to bring the rays of God's light to its readers so that they turn from a selfish, hateful, and dark existence to the true light and real life of God in Jesus.

Jesus urges people to believe in him before it is too late. *While you have the light, believe in the light, so that you may become children of light.* In Jesus' lifetime Jesus is challenging his hearers to choose light rather than darkness. He is giving people the opportunity to believe in the light and to be agents of the light. Beyond Jesus' lifetime John's Gospel continues to challenge its readers to *become children of light*, to be guided by the true light and to reveal the true light in their lives. Yes, the apostle Paul who himself turned from darkness to light puts it well: *For once you were darkness, but now in the Lord you are light. Live as children of light.(Ephesians 5:8)*

Believers ancient and modern still have time in this life, but not necessarily much time, to make their decision to get going with Jesus while the going is good, to escape the impending doom, and to become *children of light*. Beware of walking into the sunset!

Summary In John 12 Jesus and the disciples are facing a crisis. He tells a parable of crisis, the parable of the walker at sunset. Jesus is conscious that his ministry is drawing to a close. He compares day and night. He urges people to believe in him before it is too late. Believers ancient and modern still have time in this life, but not necessarily much time, to escape the impending doom, and to become *children of light.*

Connections

(a) William Temple has written: 'It is by trusting in and living by whatever light we have that we become sensitive to fuller light.'
* What are some rays of light we have in our earthly lifetime?
(b) A prisoner of the Nazis left these words etched on the wall of his cell: 'I believe in the sun even when it is not shining. I believe in love where feeling is not. I believe in God even if he is silent.'
* What are some forms of darkness which threaten believers?
(c) Frederick Buechner wrote a prayer for his dying brother: 'Dear Lord, Bring me through darkness into light. Bring me through pain into peace. Bring me through death into life. Be with me wherever I go, and with everyone I love. In Christ's name I ask it. Amen.'
* What choices are there for people who consider the words of Jesus about believing in the light?

Time for Prayer

Lord, we thank you that we have received the new life Jesus offers and do not remain lost in the darkness. Help us to walk in the light, and to believe in the light of Jesus all our days. Amen.

18 The Bathtub and the Basin

Sometimes we say that someone is throwing out the baby with the bathwater. This is a colloquial way of saying that someone is tossing out what is valued along with what is considered to be rubbish. There may be occasions when someone makes an erroneous estimation of what is to be valued or what is to be considered rubbish. As we shall see, Simon Peter's reactions to a surprising act by Jesus turn out to be over reactions and lay him open to the charge of throwing out the baby with the bathwater.

Key Text

One who has bathed does not need to wash,
except for the feet,
but is entirely clean.
(John 13:10)

Context of Key Text in John 13:1-11: 'Jesus Washes the Disciples' Feet'

In John 13 Jesus begins to prepare his disciples for his departure. The surprise washing of the disciples' feet by Jesus (John 13:1- 11) leads to a discussion of the Lord's example (John 13:12-20) and then Jesus discloses his coming betrayal by one of the disciples (John 13:21-30). The parable of the bathtub and the basin is Jesus' response to Peter's reactions to the washing of the disciples' feet.

Content of Key Text

Detail   At Passover time, Jesus displays the fullness of his love for his followers. During what we call the Last Supper Jesus gets up from the table, takes off his robe, assumes the role of a servant, and begins to wash the disciples' feet and to wipe them. Only John's Gospel records the footwashing. However, it is in tenor with the portrayal of Jesus in the other Gospels: *But I am among you as one who serves.(Luke 22:27; compare Matthew 20:28; Mark 10:45)*

When Jesus comes to Peter, Peter says, *Lord, are you going to wash my feet?(John 13:6)* Jesus replies, *You do not know now what I am doing, but later you will understand.(John 13:7)* Peter does not understand that Jesus is the Servant King, but he will understand after Jesus has gone to God the Father.

Peter then says, *You will never wash my feet.* Jesus replies, *Unless I wash you, you have no share with me.(John 13:8)* If Peter does not allow Jesus to be his Servant King, he will not share the suffering and victory of his Teacher and Lord.

Peter then says, *Lord, not my feet only but also my hands and my head!(John 13:9)* Jesus responds, *One who has bathed does not need to wash, except for the feet, but is entirely clean.* Peter has to learn to distinguish between being completely bathed before going out to dinner and having one's dirty feet washed after walking on the way to dinner on dusty roads. The dialogue between Peter and Jesus is not about what Peter does but it is about what Jesus does.

Jesus concludes, *And you are clean, though not all of you. (John 13:10)* As the Gospel writer explains, *For he knew who was to betray him; for this reason he said, 'Not all of you are clean.' (John 13:11)* Except for the betrayer, all the other disciples are clean, because by God's grace they have made decisive commitments at the beginning to be followers of their Servant King, and because day by day they continue to grow by being helped by Jesus and by coming to know him better. So then, the parable of the bathtub and the basin is a picture of being bathed completely when we turn to God and of being washed regularly as we follow Jesus.

This fits well with the early Christian rites of initiation, baptism, and continuation, the Lord's Supper. Baptism in the New Testament is a symbol of purification, identification, and incorporation. Baptism is a sign of being cleansed and forgiven, of belonging to the people of God, and of joining the body of Christ. The Lord's Supper in the New Testament has past, present, and future significance. The Lord's Supper looks back to the death of Jesus on our behalf, enriches our experience of the presence of Jesus in our lives, and looks forward to the coming of Jesus as our king.

Summary During what we call the Last Supper Jesus gets up from the table, takes off his robe, assumes the role of a servant, and begins to wash the disciples' feet and to wipe them. The dialogue between Peter and Jesus is not about what Peter does but it is about what Jesus does. The parable of the bathtub and the basin is a picture of being bathed completely when we turn to God and of being washed regularly as we follow Jesus. This fits well with the Christian rites of baptism and the Lord's Supper.

Connections

(a) In John's Gospel Jesus says to the disciples, *You have already been cleansed by the word that I have spoken to you. (John 15:3)* and in John's First Letter the writer says, *The blood of Jesus his* (God's) *Son cleanses us from all sin.(1 John 1:7)*

* How can we spell out the picture of the bathtub as a decisive cleansing?

(b) Following Jesus may mean laying down one's life as it did for the ten twentieth century martyrs whose statues are on the west front of Westminster Abbey. Or it may mean a continuing commitment to Jesus in daily life. Elsewhere Jesus says to the disciples, *If any want to become my followers, let them deny themselves and take up their cross **daily** and follow me.(Luke 9:23)*

* How can we explain the picture of the basin as a daily renewal?

(c) William Temple offers the following stirring warning: 'We may go to Church and say our prayers and read our Bibles; the cleansing Word flows over us; but if our hearts are closed we are not cleansed.'

* How can we avoid the fate of Judas, the betrayer?

Time for Prayer

Lord, we thank you that you honour our beginnings as believers. Help us to meet the demands of going on to maturity as we look to Jesus the pioneer and perfecter of our faith. Amen.

19 The Father's House

Life in society stands and falls by the way people are functional or dysfunctional in family units. A house is not necessarily a home, but it can be. If a house has people in it who care for each other and treat each other with respect, life at home can build up and not tear down. Life in God's society operates the same way. Church groups are meant to be safe and peaceful places where people learn to trust each other as people who share the present and future in the company of the Lord of the Church.

Key Text

In my Father's house there are many dwelling places.
If it were not so,
would I have told you that I go to prepare a place for you?
And if I go and prepare a place for you,
I will come again and will take you to myself,
so that where I am, there you may be also.
(John 14:2-3)

Context of Key Text in John 14:1-3, 25-27: 'Do not let your hearts be troubled'

The statement about *my Father's house* comes after an interchange between Peter and Jesus. Peter had said, *Lord, where are you going?(John 13:36)* Jesus replied that Peter could not follow him now but he would follow later. Peter asked why not because he was willing to lay down his life for Jesus. Then Jesus predicted Peter's denial. In this context Jesus gives promises to all his disciples, including Peter.

Content of Key Text

Detail   Jesus uses the words *In my Father's house* in twin circumstances. The group is near the Temple which Jesus had called *my Father's house (John 2:16)*. The group is also meeting for the Last Supper in *a large room upstairs* which Jesus calls *my guest room (Mark 14:14-15)*.

When Jesus gathers with his disciples they are worshippers in the New Temple where people worship God in Spirit, God's kind of life enjoyed by believers, and in Truth, the single basis of God's kind of life in Jesus. As Jesus had said, *The hour is coming, and is now here, when the true worshipers will worship the Father in spirit and truth.(John 4:23)*

Jesus also may be turning the meeting in the upper room into a parable of eternity. The upper room could foreshadow the heavenly home of God. Jesus says to the disciples, *I go to prepare a place for you ... I will come again and will take you to myself, so that where I am, there you may be also.*

The other Gospels and Paul tell us that Jesus had his Last Supper with the disciples in the upper room. An important element of that meal the night before Jesus died was a future reference. Christians continued to remember Jesus in bread and wine and, according to Paul, *as often as you eat this bread and drink the cup, you proclaim the Lord's death until he comes.(1 Corinthians 11:26)*

Jesus talks about *many dwelling places*. To say *many* is to say that there are enough for all. The word translated *dwelling places* has two associations. In the present Jesus can be referring to wayside shelters at stages along the road of life. Jesus goes ahead of his people and makes arrangements for resting places. This interpretation implies that if we are travelling in a heavenly direction, we are already in the Father's heavenly home.

In the future Jesus can be referring to a permanent abiding place in the sense of abiding with God. This understanding means that communion with God is a permanent and universal possibility. One is reminded of the vision of another John, the seer of Patmos, the vision of a new heaven and a new earth in which *the home of God is among mortals.(Revelation 21:2)*

Jesus is preparing *dwelling places* by preparing people who are to dwell in them. We have the blessed assurance that Jesus has already brought heaven to earth for us. We also have the blessed hope that he will make all things new. Meanwhile, Jesus promises that *the Advocate, the Holy Spirit, whom the Father will send in my name, will teach you everything, and remind you of all that I have said to you. Peace I leave with you; my peace I give to you ... Do not let your hearts be troubled, and do not let them be afraid.(John 14:26-27)*

Summary Jesus uses the words *In my Father's house* near the Temple which he had called *my Father's house* and in the upper room where Jesus had his Last Supper with the disciples. Jesus talks about *many dwelling places* with a present association of wayside shelters at stages along the road of life and with a future association of a permanent abiding place. Meanwhile, Jesus promises believers the Holy Spirit and his peace.

Connections

(a) A football coach announced his resignation. He gave two reasons: illness and fatigue. The fans had become sick and tired of him! Yet the stresses of life confront us all: changes, family life, work loads, injury or sickness. If we are seekers after mature faith life provides plenty of experiences for putting faith into practice.
* Why are followers of Jesus, then and now, troubled?
(b) The supports of Christian faith can be known in the regular patterns of home, work, sports, hobbies, worship, and study. These supports can also be available in the crises of life during pregnancy and birth, childhood and adolescence, courtship and marriage, employment and unemployment, old age and death.
* How can we, like the disciples, experience the many dwelling places in the Father's house?
(c) In classical Greek peace meant the cessation of war or strife. In the Old Testament it related to the restoration of harmony between God and humankind. In the New Testament it included objectively the peace with God (the forgiveness of the truly sorry sinner reconciled to God through Christ) and subjectively the peace of God (the tranquillity of heart and mind resulting from the Holy Spirit's assurance of reconciliation with God).
* How does Jesus give peace of mind?

Time for Prayer

Lord, give us your peace and refreshment along our path through life. Thank you for the assurance of the Spirit of truth that as we travel heavenwards we are already in heaven. Amen.

20 The Woman in Childbirth

I remember very well the births of my son and daughter. When my son was born, I waited outside the delivery room until I was summoned to see my wife and our handsome baby boy. However, when my daughter was born, I was allowed to be present, to hold my wife's hand, to encourage her as she gave birth to our beautiful baby daughter. At first hand I learned that a mother forgets the pain of childbirth as she rejoices in the safe arrival of a healthy child.

Key Text

When a woman is in labour, she has pain,
because her hour has come.
But when her child is born,
she no longer remembers the anguish because of the joy of
having brought a human being into the world.
(John 16:21)

Context of Key Text in John 16:16-24: 'Sorrow will turn into Joy'

Jesus is preparing his disciples in John 13-17 for his coming departure. They will have to face life beyond his death (John 18- 19) and resurrection (John 20-21). The parable of the woman in labour is in the context of helpful statements about the work of the Holy Spirit (John 16:4b-15) and the victory of Jesus (John 16:25-33). In John 16:16-24 Jesus promises sorrowful joy. The conquest of evil comes in the midst of conflict.

Content of Key Text

Detail   The parable of the woman in childbirth has the following format: When A occurs (*a woman is in labour ... has pain, because her hour has come*), then B occurs (*her child is born, she no longer remembers the anguish*), because C has occurred (*the joy of having brought a human being into the world*).

The structure of the parable of the woman in childbirth resembles the parable of the strong man in Luke 11:21-22. Both parables are the words of Jesus, the master wordsmith, whose utterances are unforgettable.

The parable of the woman in childbirth draws on human experience at the time of the birth of a child. People can identify with the thoughts and feelings of proud parents, especially of the mother.

The parable also draws upon the Old Testament. Isaiah of Babylon spoke of the exiles returning to Jerusalem in terms of childbirth: *a woman with child ... when she is near her time (Isaiah 26:17)* and *as soon as Zion was in labour she delivered her children (Isaiah 66:8)*. Interestingly, both Isaianic passages give hints of joy: *Your dead shall live, their corpses shall rise. O dwellers in the dust, awake and sing for joy!(Isaiah 26:19)* and *You shall see, and your heart shall rejoice (Isaiah 66:14)*. After the parable of the woman in childbirth Jesus alludes to Isaiah 66:14 when he says, *So you have pain now; but I will see you again, and your hearts will rejoice (John 16:22)*. Of course, this makes sense in the light of Jesus' death and resurrection, as well as his second coming.

The figure of birth pangs is not only evident in Isaiah 26:17 and 66:8, but it is also utilised by Jesus: *This is but the beginning of the birth pangs ... in those days there will be suffering ... after that suffering ... they will see 'the Son of Man coming in clouds' with great power and glory.(Mark 13:8,19, 24, 26)* There was the expectation of trials and tribulations before the coming of the Day of the Lord in the Old Testament and of the Son of Man in the New Testament.

The parable of the woman in childbirth has an immediate and distant focus. On the one hand, it relates to the death and resurrection of Jesus. The *pain* and *anguish* of the crucifixion of Jesus give way to the *joy* of the resurrection of the Son of God. On the other hand, it refers to the final victory of God at the second coming of Jesus, the Son of God. The *pain* and *anguish* of the Messiah's people give way to the *joy* of the Messiah's triumph.

Just as the woman suffers *pain* and *anguish* for the sake of *joy* at the safe arrival of her child, so Jesus and his followers suffer evil and death with the sure and certain hope of the victory of God in the immediate and distant future.

Summary The format of the parable of the woman in childbirth is as follows: When A occurs, then B occurs, because C has occurred. The parable draws on human experience at the time of the birth of a child. It also draws upon the Old Testament. The parable relates to the death and resurrection of Jesus and refers to the final victory of God at the second coming of Jesus.

Connections

(a) Britain's wartime Prime Minister, Winston Churchill, could easily have given up during the Battle of Britain. Yet in the dark hours of May 1940 he issued the challenge to his suffering citizens, 'I have nothing to offer but blood, toil, tears and sweat.'
* Is there no gain without pain in every day life?
(b) Oscar Romero was a bishop who identified with the poor and the persecuted in El Salvador. He said, 'I must tell you as a Christian, I do not believe in death without resurrection. If I am killed, I shall arise in the Salvadoran people.' He was shot dead in a church service on March 24, 1980. His memory is cherished by his fellow Salvadorans.
* How does a follower of Jesus see pain give way to joy?
(c) Oscar Cullmann suggested that the death and resurrection of Jesus is D-Day and it precedes V-Day, the final victory of God in the second coming of Jesus. June 6, 1944 was D-Day, the date of the Normandy invasion by the Allies. It was a decisive event which assured that complete and final victory was drawing nearer. V-Day was a day nominated to celebrate victory. May 8, 1945, V-E Day (Victory in Europe), followed Germany's surrender.
* What do we think about the explanation of God's victory in Jesus in terms of D-Day and V-Day?

Time for Prayer

Lord, we think of the death of Jesus as the necessary precursor to his resurrection. Help us to endure the lows of life and then to enjoy the highs of life here and hereafter. Amen.

Postscript

At the end of my musings and meditations on the word pictures in John's Gospel I am drawn to a prayer of Kierkegaard reprinted in *The Fount Book of Prayer*. It seems to capture the spirit of the portrait of Jesus according to John.

The Fourth Evangelist writes out of the Jewish world into the Roman world at the end of the first century. Jesus the Jew is the Saviour of the world. He transcends time and place and yet belongs to a particular time and place. In the second decade of the twenty-first century the personal affirmations Jesus makes and the parables Jesus speaks in John's Gospel still ring true.

I invite my readers to pray with Søren Kierkegaard, the Danish philosopher, who lived between 1813 and 1855 and devoted his life to exploring what it is to be a follower of Jesus.

O Lord Jesus Christ,
I love to live in your presence,
to see your human form and to watch you walking on earth.
I do not want to see you
through the darkened glass of tradition,
nor through the eyes of today's values and prejudices.
I want to see you as you were,
as you are,
and as you always will be.
I want to see you as an offence to human pride,
as a man of humility,
walking among the lowliest of men and women,
and yet as the Saviour and Redeemer of the human race.
Amen.

For God so loved the world that he gave his only Son, so that everyone who believes in him may not perish but may have eternal life.

John 3:16

Select Bibliography

A Prayer Book for Australia (Broughton Books, 1998)
Barclay, William. *The Daily Study Bible: The Gospel of John Vols. 1 & 2* (Saint Andrew Press, 1975)
Barrett, C. K. *The Gospel according to St. John Second Edition* (Westminster, 1978)
Brown, Raymond E. *The Gospel according to John Vols. 1 & 2* (Doubleday, 1966, 1974)
Buechner, Frederick. *Beyond Words* (HarperSanFrancisco, 2004)
_____ *The Eyes of the Heart* (HarperSanFrancisco, 1999)
Bultmann, Rudolf. *The Gospel of John* (Blackwell, 1971)
Culpepper, R. Alan. *The Gospel and Letters of John* (Abingdon, 1998)
_____ *Anatomy of the Fourth Gospel* (Fortress, 1983)
Dodd, C. H. *The Interpretation of the Fourth Gospel* (Cambridge, 1953)
_____ *Historical Tradition in the Fourth Gospel* (Cambridge, 1963)
Harner, Philip B. *The "I Am" of the Fourth Gospel* (Fortress Press, 1970)
Hinson, E. Glenn. *A Serious Call to a Contemplative Lifestyle* (Smyth & Helwys, 1993)
Hull, William E. 'John,' *The Broadman Bible Commentary*, 9:189-376 (Broadman, 1970)
Hunter, A. M. *According to John* (SCM, 1968)
Lincoln Andrew T. *The Gospel according to Saint John* (Hendrickson, 2005)
Lyall, Frank. *The "I Am" Sayings of Jesus* (Mentor, 1996)
Morris, Leon L. *The Gospel According to John* (Eerdmans, 1991)
Morton, H. V. *In the Steps of the Master* (Rich & Cowan, 1934)
O'Day, Gail R. 'The Gospel of John,' *The New Interpreter's Bible*, 9:491-865 (Abingdon, 1995)
Partington, Angela. Editor. *The Oxford Dictionary of Quotations* (Oxford, 1996)
Rowston, Doug. *A Bird's Eye View of the Bible* (MediaCom, 2007)
Schweizer, Eduard. 'What about the Johannine Parables?'
Exploring the Gospel of John In Honor of D. Moody Smith, pp 208-19
Edited by R. Alan Culpepper & C. Clifton Black (WJKP, 1996)
Smith, D. Moody. *John* (Abingdon, 1999)
Temple, William E. *Readings in St. John's Gospel* (Macmillan, 1952)
Van de Weyer, Robert. Editor. *The Fount Book of Prayer* (HarperCollins, 1993)
Witherington, III, Ben. *John's Wisdom* (John Knox, 1995)
Wright, Tom. *John for Everyone Parts 1 and 2* (SPCK, 2002)

Dr Doug Rowston lives in Adelaide, South Australia, with his wife Rosalie and their noble canine a Welsh Corgi dog. He is a Baptist Minister who has worked as theological lecturer at Burleigh College, religious education teacher at Prince Alfred College, pastor of Richmond Baptist Church, and adjunct lecturer at St Barnabas College (Charles Sturt University).

Doug has also written *A Bird's Eye View of the Bible (Second Edition); Pray and Sing: Prayers & Songs in the New Testament; Promises & Blessings in the Book of Revelation; Things that Jesus said: Parables of the Kingdom & Eternal Life; Things that Jesus did: Miracles of the Kingdom & Signs of Eternal Life; From Unread to Misread: Hebrews to Revelation Neglected New Testament Books.*

www.ingramcontent.com/pod-product-compliance
Lightning Source LLC
Chambersburg PA
CBHW030302010526
44107CB00053B/1787